Dedication:

I am forever grateful for my ancestors, whose wisdom immensely enriched my life. Also, this book is dedicated to all of those who seek to overcome the challenging obstacles life brings.

ii

PURSUIT
— OF THE —
SOUL

Allowing Your Perfect Life Journey

AVERY ALEXANDER

*The author is a holistic practitioner with over
20 years experience and research into mind, body
and soul medicine. She is a medical intuitive and spiritual life coach who has helped thousands find their
way back home. To ultimately find oneself is
the pursuit of the soul.*

Table of Contents

Table of Contents Continued Next Page

Table of Contents Continued

Acknowledgments

To Grandmas Leila, Lula, Susan and Sylvia rest on til' we meet again. Thank you Dorian, who never complained and said "I would not take nothing for the journey."

I wish to send heartfelt thanks and acknowledgement (although too numerous to name) to all of those who believed in me and this work.

Love to Mom Linda and Dad John.

A special thank you to Art Ferdig for all your wonderful encouragement and direction in bringing forth this book.

I also acknowledge you readers, all those facing challenges, physical or otherwise, and for anyone who is or has been deathly sick and needs encouragement. May your life experience a new wellness and expedient transformation. I trust you will enjoy and benefit from these pages. I invite you to share your thoughts and comments by emailing me, Avery Alexander (spiritual name *SaEnya*), at saenya@yahoo.com.

*"Your mind is your garden; your thoughts
are your seeds. You will harvest
either flowers or weeds."*
Author Unknown

Introduction

This book came about after much discussion and coaxing by my patients, friends and support group who appreciate these insights and wisdom on wellness.

Where does illness come from? I am going to make a radical statement about wellness, one that may not be accepted by the current medical establishment and model. This is what I have discovered from over fifteen years of observation and integrative practice with people from around the globe. Illness begins first in the thoughts, then it manifest in the emotions. By the time illness manifests in the physical, it has already been developing for months and even years.

The physical manifestation is simply an out picturing or a display of what has been happening in the psyche. The illness whispers in our thoughts like a seed blowing in the wind, wanting to take root. Once the illness *thought-seed* has taken root, it begins to grow and the volume gets louder as it manifests in the emotions. The *thought-seed* of illness begins to grow like a tree. Its roots grow deeper into the soil of the mind and continues until it manifests in the body. Now it has become what I would call an expressed illness, shouting "I am here!" At this point the illness cannot be denied. The symptoms of the physical are too loud to ignore. At this stage, the current medical model states the person has a disease. But, I say disease occurs long before this in the invisible realm.

It is the within, the subtle realm, where I look first.   I declare there are invisible and visible illnesses. This is the premise of this book, *Pursuit of the Soul*. We must first identify the diseases of the soul, heal them and create a whole life from that awareness.

There are progressions of illness. Like every manifestation, they first begin in the unseen realm then progress to the 'seen' realm. It then behooves the one who has manifested the illness to seek where there is discomfort, first in thought, then emotion and then the physical body. Then one can find the root and trace the disease and illness. Do not be complacent with any type of illness at any level. Be like the prudent gardener who everyday seeks out the weeds and plucks them out. A wise gardener knows it is futile to cut the weed above ground where it is seen for it will only grow back thicker and taller than before. To eliminate the weed the gardener must pluck it out from where it is not seen, by the roots. This is where it begins to grow in the first place.

Like the wise gardener, we must constantly look at our lives and embrace inner development. We can then insure a life more beautiful than even the most arrayed gardens.

Avery Alexander
(SaEnya)

Forward

Having a good name is better than silver and gold, for it is a key to unlocking one's destiny. My birth name means the truth and that is what I am about, revealing truths no matter how unusual they may seem.

My calling is to assist and elevate the health of people. What I have discovered is very simple: when one follows one's purpose it leads to wellness. Refusing to follow one's purpose leads to dis-ease.

Seeking to know *how* and *why* we were created leads to knowledge and wisdom. Ignorance of this knowledge, from my observation, leads to sickness. Anything that does not follow the natural purpose of why it was created will eventually destroy itself.

One of my goals in life is to elevate awareness that life is a perfect experience and that everything happens for a reason. We are becoming who we are by shifting and changing our consciousness daily. We shift through our thinking. We change by our actions.

It is the ability to dream and focus on who and what we are that makes us unique in comparison to animals.

Ever since I can remember, I've been able to meld into or enter into other realms and worlds through my imagination. I been able to extract information about people and circumstances through visions and dreams. The energies, I recognized, were from another place and time. I shared some of these things as a child with my Grandma, she accepted me wholeheartedly.

My Grandma allowed me to play in these unseen realms all the time. These other realms can best be described as the unconscious mind or the mind behind the curtain. It became second nature to me to engage that mind or other awareness. It is subtle awareness we are born with. It is the ability to extract information without knowing why.

My maternal Grandmother was a natural healer, a descendant of African and Seminole Native Americans from Florida. My paternal Grandma was Blackfoot Indian and African American from South Carolina. Both Grandmas used natural herbs and remedies to heal my maladies. As a little girl, holding on to my paternal Grandmother's apron in her herbal and food garden, I watched how she used earthly concoctions to make medicine not only for me but other folks nearby. From both Grandmas, I learned firsthand about observation in natural healing and remedies. I watched them use certain herbs and techniques that always seemed to work and made me whole again. I honor my Grandmothers, for they always allowed me to be myself. It would be wonderful if all children were nurtured in this way to keep their beliefs open. I accepted my ability to relate to spirit as a gift from the Creator.

I believe my intent to help others and the planet is why I was able to get information from my visions and dreams. In my visions I would speak with

Angels. I would envision them working and flying around in a heavenly sphere. Sometimes they would speak to me, not out loud, but through my mind, about people and circumstances.

What I shared through dreams would come to pass in a matter of three to six months. I had a dream that the next door neighbor was expecting a baby. A few months later she was. She had a girl. I dreamed the police officer down the street was in jail. Six months later he was, for raping a young woman. At age six I dreamed my maternal Grandmother would die when I reached the age of fifteen. This happened as foretold.

Not all information given to me was a prediction, as some came in the form of counsel. The information I received was inspiring and led me to connect with a higher power. I always felt elevated and it helped me see life from a different perspective. From this, I developed a deep appreciation and love for the Divine Creator. I would find myself praying and talking with the Creator of all life. What a Joy! Communicating on that level felt very comfortable. I was young, true, but I believed in everything I was experiencing. I was made aware that I was communicating with celestial beings.

The knowledge was so profound. It seemed perfectly normal for me, and I thought everyone had their own guardian angels that talked with them as well. But as the years passed, to my surprise, I discovered that talking with celestial beings through visions and dreams was not the case for everyone. I felt my childhood prayers were heard in earnest. I always prayed with faith that my prayers would be answered. Every time I would ask, my prayers seemed to be answered in one way or another. This led me to believe that I was a part of something greater. I felt comfort in knowing that my requests were being heard.

As one grows older, beliefs of society can wash away natural, youthful intuition. They can alter how one is truly designed to be. Truth always presents itself in our life even if we choose not to recognize it. In our younger years, truth of spirit can be very much a part of us. As we grow older, society's norms seem to crowd out the simple truths of youth.

Since I was five, I knew I wanted to be a nurse. This set the course for my life. I studied natural medicine in NYC and later in the Caribbean.

Holistic remedies felt natural for me to use. Blending the best of traditional medicine with effective non-traditional medicine is like mixing a finely blended drink; once you have the right combination, any disease can be conquered. In native medicine and the practice of holistic remedies one must believe and know about the unseen, subtle realms. One must be able to work and extract information from various sources. True healing comes from healing subtle energies that interact with the dis-eased person. Most folks would call this being intuitive.

This is what I truly am, a medical intuitive. Gathering information from unseen realms is like tuning your television to gather insight from different channels. Once tuned into the frequency, the broadcast is easily accessed. It is like turning your mind to the station that is downloading the information about the person or the health issue. The body's energy will usually tell you everything you need to know to heal it if one listens and observes what the body's reaction is. It is important to notice the body's reaction.

I discovered when disease is present there tends to be a disconnection between what the person is saying or thinking and what the body is saying. True healing occurs when the Mind, Body and Spirit are aligned with one voice or message.

The main key I discovered for true healing is observation of the body. The body is always communicating to us with its own language. Ancient healers knew how to interpret this language, and knew that a healthy body was balanced through knowing and understanding this language. It is easily readable through observing the signs and symptoms that one exhibits. Knowing the body's secrets is important, for they hold the key to longevity. We know that how the body is managed today will determine how the body will respond in the future. We can then, by modifying the current thought patterns and habits, improve the health of the body in the months ahead. Also, based on expressed symptoms that the body has manifested, we can trace back and determine what thoughts, habits and ways of being may have caused the symptoms to manifest in the first place.

Many scientists do not fully understand what makes the body age.

Every single cell in the body regenerates itself. It takes about seven years for the body to totally regenerate itself.

On average it takes three weeks to generate a new stomach lining, and six months to generate a new liver. Everyday new bone cells and new brain cells are regenerating. I am asserting that all dis-eases of the body take root and stay in place because of one's thought, beliefs, habits and practices. All new cells in the body are subjected to the same effects that caused the old cells to manifest sickness.

Once the environment of the body has changed into a life sustaining environment, meaning the bio-chemicals and functioning that caused the dis-ease in the body dissolves; the body shifts and true healing begins to manifest. Total wellbeing for today requires a paradigm shift, a change in one's beliefs, conscious-ness, attitudes, awareness and feelings are needed. What I have been learning and teaching about natu-ral healing is my passion, it is my purpose. Through-out the book are affirmations of self — sound bites-called 'notes' to self. Use them as *thought seeds*; speaking them to yourself, preferably, out loud. Words have power to generate, create and balance the mind and body.

I wrote this book to share with you what I dis-covered in hopes that you may live a long, happy and prosperous life.

All we need is to say is YES, to life!

*Note to Self: In every moment,
I now choose to live life to
the fullest.*

Chapter 1:

New Beginnings

The year was 1991. April 19th to be exact. I was in a hospital bed racked with pain.

Earlier that morning, I had life-altering surgery. I was told before going in that this would be a 'quick day surgery' for a cyst discovered on my right ovary. The doctor assured me I would be home by 5 p.m. "All we need to do is drain the cyst off your ovary and you will be going home."

I marveled as the doctor was explaining this quick day surgery concept to me the week before, but I did not totally trust everything the doctor was telling me. I could not believe that I had this problem. I never had any symptoms. The problem was discovered by have an ordinary doctor's exam.

I did get a second opinion. The second doctor agreed and said it was best to go ahead with the surgery. I chose to proceed with the 'quick day surgery' as recommended.

Modern science I thought; imagine I can have surgery and be home in my living room after 5 p.m., perhaps in time to catch the evening news! They had looked at my ovaries two weeks earlier with a sonogram machine, using sound waves, and the doctor had determined that all I had was fluid on the right ovary. I thought it would be quick and easy.

Now to fast forward... after surgery, I lay racked with immense pain. No way was I going home today by 5 p.m.

It was way after five now and I was nowhere close to home. There were staples up and down my abdomen, and it felt like tubes are connected to me everywhere.

A morphine pump dispensed a hallucinogenic pain narcotic into my veins. A tube was stuck down my nose, draining something from my stomach, and more tubes were sticking out from my body letting me know I was not okay.

What the heck had just happened to me? It felt like I was hit by a freight train and my body invaded by robbers.

I felt like whoever stole my life, please bring it back!

Transitions

It was all too much for me. I was overwhelmed. What happened to a little cyst being drained and I would be probably propped up on my pillows at home watching the 5 p.m. news? I learned that day; five o'clock would not come for a very long time for me.

For almost a month after, I would remain in the

hospital wondering if I would ever make it home at all.

I was truly on the edge between life and death.

I did not know if I was going to get through this alive.

More Shocking News

The doctor came into my room the day after my surgery. While sitting down next to me he gazed at me with sad, pitiful eyes and explained to me that my right ovary had a tumor so big it was the size of a cantaloupe. He thought it best to remove it entirely!

I was in shock over what I heard. Did he just say he had to remove my right ovary? And that it was the size of a cantaloupe? I could not believe what I was hearing.

Also, he continued saying in a 'matter -of- fact' tone, that my left ovary also had the same tumor looking projections on it, and he felt the need to remove that one as well!

Now, I am shocked beyond belief. I was just out of college, but I felt like a child out of nursery school. As he continued talking my mind was racing with a thousand questions all at the same time. What about having another child? Were there tumors anywhere else? Was I going to live?

Oh Angels, I need you now! Talk about being devastated! My whole life, as I knew it, would never be the same again.

The doctor told me what type of tumor it was but he needed to confirm it with testing. Waiting on the tumor report was like watching time in slow motion. It took a week to find out.

It was all so crazy. My life had turned upside down in an instant. How could this have happened so suddenly?

What if he made a mistake? I was always so very healthy, or so I thought. I made sure I took care of my health by taking supplements and exercising frequently. I was a new grad from nursing school and thought I understood what I needed to do to maintain my health.

I wished they could have awakened me before removing my *stuff* out of my body. Now it was too late.

Who authorized this?

Frustration and Anger

I remember being angry, confused, and upset over the whole process. Apparently, the consent form that *I signed* authorized the doctor with the privileges to do '*whatever*.' I had not fully read the small print or understood the implications of what I had signed. I would not have agreed with it! Not one bit!

As I saw it, I signed the permission for possible 'castration'. I felt castrated if there is such a thing for a woman. Did someone say neutered? Yeah, that felt more descriptive as to what had happened.

This hospital permission paragraph was written in small print, and it was not a clear explanation of all the possibilities and powers I had signed over to the surgeon. It read, *"I give the surgeon permission to do anything deemed medically necessary."* No one ever talked about *ovary hunting* as a possibility. I did not fully understand the repercussions of the surgery consent term 'necessary'.

Apparently, I did not know as much about the medical system as I had thought. I did not see the importance of the small print, especially when I was being injected with anesthesia the time.

It is so important to get and understand all the facts!

Emptiness

Why didn't someone care to wake me up and ask me what I wanted or what I thought, since I signed for a cyst to be drained and they took out my ovaries and fallopian tubes!

"Guess what?" the surgeon said, "You can still have a child if you want- we left your womb."

I am wondering what kind of child I could have without my ovaries! I did not doubt that I could have another child, but they would not have my genetic make-up. All of my genetic make-up was now somewhere in a jar inside a cold lab with my name on it, waiting to be examined by a pathologist.

The doctor continued, "Well, we also took out some lymph nodes because you had some cancerous cells in those, too, but again this was all sent to the lab to confirm."

I would see if they did me a favor when the report comes back.

I waited for what seemed an eternal week for the pathologist report. Yes, to my relief it did confirm that I had a *stage 4 tumor on both ovaries*, and it confirmed that the lymph nodes were indeed cancerous

These cancerous cells had spread to my abdominal fluid. The surgery had proved necessary. Before then, I felt the surgeon and the pathologist were all in it together to conspire against me!

The confirmation did let me know that the surgeon had a plausible cause to do what he had done. Soon my anger turned into fear. All I could think o was that I had cancer and it had spread to my abdomen! Now the doctors are telling me I need chemotherapy.

Note to Self: Fears are "False Emotions about Reality" - SaEnya

Chapter 2:

What Next?

What a bleak story this was turning out to be. I was a young woman. Now I felt like I was ninety-nine years old! I was thrown into instant menopause. My body would undergo painful and frightening transitions that I would not want anybody to experience. I felt like I was on a freight train that was about to derail.

I went along with the chemotherapy. I did not know what else to do. Little did I know what the effects of the chemotherapy would have on my body. I was so sick from the chemotherapy that I did not have the strength to comb my hair. My hair was so thin from the chemo that you could see my scalp. I was frail, weak, and I felt I was dying. Life seemed to be slipping from my grasp.

It felt like I was dying as I lay in the hospital bed. My skin smelled like putrid poison from chemo and cancer. My frail hair smelled like old wood that had been chard in a fire. I plunged into a totally different world. I knew I would not be the same again.

Just two months before all of this, I was a strong, robust person. I jogged frequently and exercised. Now, I could hardly put one foot in front of the other by myself! I had no strength. I could barely move. I could not put on make-up, nor did I feel any zest for life. My vibrancy had left. My hope for living had very much diminished.

A Limited World

While lying in the hospital bed my mind flashed back to when I was eight years old. Rice was flying everywhere as my Mom and her new husband were descending down the stairs and out of my Aunt Mary's and Uncle John's house. My mom was a newlywed for the first time. She looked happy and relieved that she had met her true love.

My new stepdad was very unusual to say the least. After being married for three months he started to share his weird thoughts with me. One day out of the blue he said in a blunt tone, "You know I do not believe in God. God does not exist." I stared at him in disbelief how can this guy *not believe in God?!* Is he crazy or what! That means he can't believe in Angels either. Hum? I had to investigate this further.

Being an inquisitive and analytical child I said to him, "Well, if you do not believe in God, that means you do not believe in the Angels or the Devil either." Then he began to explain that after seeing his best friend in combat in Vietnam get blown into pieces before his very eyes, he made up his mind right then and there that God could not possibly exist. My stepdad in his low monotone voice stated: "If there is a God *why would he permit all this evil to go on in the world? Why do people die and suffer the way that they do?*"

I could not answer him. I did not know why. He made sense in what he believed. In my current state, I laid there wondering why God would allow me to get sick. *Why did this suffering come upon me?* I thought, right now I really need God to exist. I need help.

I remember my stepdad opening his old, rusty file cabinet and taking out every piece of evidence that he could find to try to prove to me that God really *does not* exist. He also went over to his book cabinet and pulled books off the shelf as the dust was floating in the air.

"What's this?" I asked, sneezing emphatically.

"You need to read these; it will show you about this 'so called God.' You will learn it was all made up."

I believed whole heartedly in God. I went to Catholic school five days of the week saying 'Hail Mary's' and 'Our Fathers' prayers until I was convinced I would become a Nun.

Only I did not notice any Nun that looked like me.

My Grandmother made sure I was at the Baptist Church on Sundays with my hat and white gloves on. If there was anyone who was steeped into being religious it was me.

Everyone I ever knew believed in God, except my weird stepdad. As far as I saw it, he was crossing a dangerous line straight into hell! He even went on to say, "Have you ever seen God?" in a mocking tone, trying to convince me more.

"No," I sheepishly responded.

"Well, how do you know God exists?"

"I just know that He does." I responded.

"I bet you believe in the Tooth Fairy and Santa Clause too!"

"Well, I do!" I proudly exclaimed, as any child would say at that age.

To me it was tooth and nothing but the tooth, so help me...who?

With his words, I felt the innocence veil of my childhood tearing apart.

He continued to give me evidence of his theories: The Big Bang Theory, Charles Darwin, The Evolution of Man, Easter Island and the Alien theory. Amen came from Egypt. Constantine the father of Christianity created that religion after visiting and following after the Egyptian stories. Constantine the father of Christianity created that religion three hundred years after Christ had died, visiting and following after the Egyptian stories.

The Immaculate Conception did have stark similarities to the Egyptian version. Isis (Auset) the Divine Mother birthed Horus (Heru) to reclaim his Father Osiris's (Ausar's) lost kingdom. Heru's conception was done by spiritual means. The kingdom was overthrown by his evil brother Set (Sebek). Heru grew up and returned the Kingdom back to Ausar.

Other books I read talked about the Bermuda triangle, strange disappearances, and crop circles appearances from Aliens.

He began to tell me about the ancient civilizations such as the Mayans, the ancient Atlantians, and more on the Egyptians. He pointed to pictures in books as he showed me what to read to prove everything he was saying.

"No, I never heard of this stuff" I said, as I was thinking what else didn't I know about? "Where did you get this stuff from? And why do you think what you are saying is true? Is it is true?" I continuously asked him until he responded.

"True knowledge is often hidden from the masses; they limit information to keep people ignorant." Then he went on to say, "I collected information over the years because I could not believe everything people were telling me."

He continued, "God is a theory because no one has ever produced any evidence that God actually exists."

He continued, "Charles Darwin stated man evolved from Apes. So there goes the Adam and Eve story. Scientists proved it took billions of years for the Earth to form, not seven days like it says in the Bible."

"So what happens to people when they die", I asked. "Don't they go to heaven?" I questioned him more intently.

"There is no such thing." He looked me in the eye without blinking and continued speaking as if he was a major authority on the subject.

"It was all made up to control people and society," he replied. "If you had slaves would you teach them information that could set them free?"

"I guess not. If they were free they would I not have slaves anymore" I said.

"Ahh,' he had a wide-mouth grin as he spoke and said, "the religion you have came from Slave owners. Isn't that true?"

"I guess so?" I said with a frown on my face. "So, what happens to my soul, I pray every night to God for my Soul to keep like Grandma taught me?" I was now speaking in a pleading tone.

Please God say it is not true, I want to believe in you, I thought to myself.

He continued saying in a bleak tone, "There is no soul, when you die, you just die. You go into the ground and earthworms eat your body and that's it!"

Well, to me that was not a pleasant answer at all. *I began thinking what if he was telling the truth?*

"Sorry kid, that's just the facts. No need of me sugar coating the truth."

This to me was the response of a mad-man. It was the beginning of my critical thinking. I began to question everything. This was a gift to begin to question. It started my intense passion for seeking. It is through questioning, one gains awareness of the soul. Does it exist? The Supreme Being whom I was told is God – does this being exist? I accepted before what everyone told me. This shift now shook everything down to my core. This event caused me to know for sure if what I was told is true.

Ground Zero

I was curious. I kept on asking him questions. I was fascinated with these new concepts – aliens from outer space, ancient civilizations, science. The more I asked, the more he shared.

In the past, when I asked an adult a question, they would 'shoo' me away or give me some hurried up answer. I guess my many questions would become aggravating after a while.

I used to ask so many questions it would fray the nerves of any sane person. But with my stepdad I had an adult in front of me who was willing to answer all of my questions in detail and show me books and literature to back up what he was saying. He was someone who would answer all of my thousands of questions at length. As I finished one book, he gave me another to read. My mind was ablaze with learning new knowledge. It felt expansive and empowering to understand the cosmos of the world I lived in. My eager mind absorbed all these new philosophies like a sponge. It wasn't too long after, that I was doing my own research.

Questions About God

I concluded with him that perhaps there wasn't a God; at least not in the way I was taught to believe. God was a male dominated God, who was jealous and you dare not question Him. That did not seem to work for a kid who had a passion for curiosity. If I am not to question God then why would God make me to be curious? I had to admit, some things did not add up. Why would God be jealous and vengeful as I was taught? Why would God create humans then repent as If he made a mistake in creating man? Then wipe them all out but a select few? If God was all-seeing and all-knowing, would not he have known Eve was going to eat the forbidden fruit in the garden?

Why would God put a tree in the Garden of Eden for them not to touch and eat? When the fact is mankind is curious by nature. I could imagine the tree is there tempting them night and day; like 'ahah you cannot eat of me.' All of these things did not make sense to me as a young child.

Whenever I asked an adult about these things they all seemed to give me that mysterious answer. No matter who answered, whether it was from Grandmas, to Mom, to Granddads, to the Nuns or the Priest.

They would say, "You are not to question God."

My motto became something like this: If you cannot see it then it does not exist.

I was grateful and privileged to have knowledge that most kids my age never knew. I think I grew up before my time. While most kids were out playing hop scotch and dolly, I was up in my room trying to figure out the Cosmos and God's existence. Perhaps they never thought about it. But I did. My whole life became an inquiry to know the truth. Is God real?

I did not know why, perhaps it was the powerful influence of my stepdad, but I began losing my convictions about God. Inside I felt my existence was bleak and the zest for life was sort of gone. Was it because I lost my belief in God? Had I lost something that I could hope in and believe in? I stopped talking to my celestial friends. I had knowledge but I did not feel inspired. The inspirational messages I had once received had stopped. No more inspirational dreams. I did not believe in it anymore. Before, I had looked forward to knowing the Divine Creator; now to me it was all a myth. All I had to look forward to in the end was earth worms? The very thought sickened me.

What was there to believe in anymore? I had changed as my beliefs changed.

Note to Self: Belief kill and belief cure. (An old Jamaican saying.)

The Spark

Months later I was riding on the Main Street bus in Buffalo; the sun was beaming through the tree lined streets. The trees seemed to sparkle as the sunlight touched the leaves. I noticed particularly how the sun filtered through the trees and I saw how the wind began to gently blow through the leaves.

Time seemed to slow down just a bit. I opened the bus window to allow more of the sultry breeze to flow through. As, I felt the gentle caress of the wind, a thought came to me that would set things in motion and would change my life forever.

Designer in the Design

I began to go deep in thought. I noticed how the trees, sun, and wind danced with each other. The trees also seemed to interact with the wind and the sun so perfectly. Then a thought hit me like a bright light in the head, 'the wind!'

My reasoning began taking a different perspective. "I cannot see the wind, yet I see a moving, invisible real force through the trees, ruffling the leaves, moving in an easterly direction."

My mind began to race; perhaps, there was a designer who designed the wind. This took my mind beyond my current belief of: *if I could not see it, it did not exist.* Then I thought, "Whoever, designed the

31

wind could be invisible too! Perhaps, I could feel the designer like I feel the wind? Not everything that is real is visible to the naked eye. I learned that day that observation of what is can be visible and invisible. So, *how do I now learn more about the invisible?*

I concluded not to rely on external senses to figure out the existence of a Supreme Being. I needed to search out more knowledge. It was so perfect the way the wind danced with trees. I gathered things are present because the designer created it so.

Then, I continued to follow on that train of thought. This very seat I am sitting on had someone to design it for it to function and for it to be present. The trees perhaps have a designer too, because trees have a function and they are present. The trees are too perfect to be a random spoof of the universal big bang... I concluded, there must be another world other than what I am able to see.

The stream of thought was abruptly interrupted, "LAST STOP!" the bus driver shouted from around the giant bus wheel. I arose; I felt my heart began to expand with all the possibilities of discovering another reality. It all started to make sense to me.

As I walked down the street to my house, I created a plan to find the Creator. If the Creator existed, I was determined to find this being. If there is a Creator who designed the trees, I want to know the real truth. *And if the designer is alive like the wind with movement, I will find the truth!*

I was being initiated into a new life, my powerful, awesome life and did not realize it! A string of events would be the beginning, not the end, to life as I knew it.

These events triggered by the later illness would be the catalyst to greater access in life. Like the wind triggered a new set of events in a little girl's search for the Divine Creator. I found the truth always is there. By opening my eyes and observing what is so in nature, it changed my life and set me on the path of discovering inner truth.

I later came to see the way out of pain, suffering and poverty is knowledge that can be applied. All knowledge is not truthful information. The key to distinguishing truth from falsity is within; it is a gift of awareness, the ability to listen to your inner self. I will distinguish that in another chapter.

In Search of Truth

At home that night, after my bus-ride experience, I closed my eyes tight and began to ask silently in my mind God, Creator, and Most High whatever you are called by – the Divine force that made the wind and everything that exists – if you do exist, please reveal yourself to me! Let me know the truth!

It had been long time since I prayed. I felt a little awkward talking to something I could not see. I had a 'light bulb' moment. How did I change from a little girl believing in a Higher Power and Celestial Beings, to becoming an Atheist at another point? I decided I would search for truth and it would be revealed. Truth is not based on beliefs.

If the Supreme Being does exist, I was hoping my communication got through and that this Being would respond to me.

The desire to know more about this life and the truth began to burn in my heart. I began to feel and notice more about nature. If, there is a Creator then nature is a reflection of its design.

I began to study science, astronomy, human beings and nature. Like a master sleuth, I was out gathering clues of evidence. In studying the creation there were clues about the Creator.

That night I had a vivid dream in beautiful colors. *I was walking through a thick beautiful forest and in the center was a big rock for me sit on. I sat down and out of nowhere appeared a tall elegant woman dressed in white linen. Her skin was golden; her hair was tied up in a twist hairstyle. I asked her, "Can you tell me about God?"*

She looked at me and said, "There is a force that exists in everything. It permeates through every single being and non-being. What you seek is inside of you and all around you. You are it and it is you."

Then she smiled and disappeared as easily as she had appeared. I awoke that morning with a smile and a feeling that I was a little closer to finding the truth.

Note to Self: Be observant - all the answers are there. I can know everything about life by observing what is and what is now.

Chapter 3:

Good Friends are Like Medicine

In my cold, darkly lit hospital room, it seemed like my whole world was crashing around me. I had too much time on my hands; all I could do was reflect on life and what I was now enduring.

It made my mind race and my stomach crunch into knots. Thinking about my current circumstances made a deep feeling rise up out of the pit of my stomach. I always wanted to contribute something meaningful to the world. I always wanted to make a difference.

Now, that seemed all down the drain. Now, I lay in the hospital stricken with what I thought was a terminal disease. How did I get this? How could this happen? I thought.

I wondered if I would ever have the chance to make a difference in my life and for others. I felt out of control, and helpless. I wished I could have thought about myself more instead of wanting to help the world by being 'superwoman'. I could not help anyone in this condition, not even myself.

In my sickly condition, most of my friends were scared for me and stayed away at times, not knowing what to say or do for me.

I was upset over the fact that some of my closest friends had not visited me in the hospital. I was sad, lonely and needing reassurance. Perhaps they could not handle my grim prognosis. Needless to say I was disappointed not having the support of my friends. I also was angry and felt abandoned. I needed to change the grim stories of why these events were unfolding in my life. It did not make me feel good or empowered. The next question an inquisitive natured person like me would ask, now how exactly do I find out why I got cancer?

I began to see that life is an incredible opportunity, not given to us in vain. It is given to have awareness of life and to have it more abundantly. Everything has an advantage. I was going to refocus myself as to what the advantage of having stage four ovarian cancer was all about. I would be the phoenix rising out of the ashes.

Note to self: In pursuing purpose, become aware of what feels empowering and what doesn't. Follow wholeheartedly what empowers, and what ultimately frees the soul.

Life sometimes presents pleasant surprises. When I was so sick in the hospital for nearly a month.

I got used to, sad to say, the infrequent visitors. However, I was pleasantly surprised when an old friend whom I had not seen in a while visited me. I never expected him to be there for me, but he was, and his behavior totally caught me off guard. I will keep him nameless at this point, but if he is reading this he knows who he is! He was very nurturing to me. His humorous ways were exactly what I needed to lift me up.

I had become physically weak, and felt frozen and stiff. I needed someone to help me with the simple tasks of combing my hair, brushing my teeth, and bathing. He combed my hair; he assisted me in walking too. He brought me food when I found the hospital 'grub' not appetizing. I was very surprised at how he cared for me. He seemed before to be the opposite. Yet, it was now a healing balm to my soul. The ones I expected to be there for me never showed up; but he was exactly who I needed to get me through this difficult time.

In my frailty, I felt death breathing its icy, cold breath down my neck. As he was arranging yellow roses in a clear glass vase for me, I confessed to him, "I think, I'm dying."

My friend stopped what he was doing, and looked at me as if I cursed at him in an unknown language or something!

"Shush," he said, now looking very sternly at me. *"You will not die- you will live!"* His words reverberated through me like an earth tremor.

"Don't think about dying any more, *you will live!* Do you hear me? Only think and say you will live!"

Something about the words spoken, "YOU WILL LIVE", took root inside me. As he said it, I began to believe him. I wanted to live and embrace all what life has to offer me.

His words felt like someone revived me by breathing fresh words of encouragement into my lungs.

I wished what he said could only be that simple. How could he be so sure? At that moment, his words of confidence and strength were all I had to hold on to. By the grace of Life it was at that exact moment, *I chose to live!*

I Have the Power and Will to Live!

After surgery I could not go anywhere; my body was restricted to the hospital bed. Being restricted in the confinement of my bed was my saving grace.

It was a place to reflect and to stop the negative mind. I had to mentally stop running in fear and be with myself. Being in so much pain drove me within. Going within my inner space allowed me to escape my present physical reality.

Being confined in my outer world gave me unlimited freedom in my inner world. When I practiced going within, I visualized that I was healthy, healed, happy and fulfilled. I would imagine I was talking to my higher, the perfect Divine Self. There was a victorious, conquering feeling that came over me that allowed me to rise up and embrace life. I was transforming into someone and something stronger.

From my acceptance of allowing the Great

Good Friends are Like Medicine

Healer, within, to move on my behalf, I feel I attracted two more unexpected visitors: Skipper and his girl-friend, Mindy. They prayed for me. We joined hands and agreed for my divine healing. They were wonderful. I started to feel much better afterwards.

When I asked my doctor if there was any cure for healing the cancer, he said, "No."

With his answer, I began to wonder, why is it that man could put a rocket in space but the only option to cancer is to poison it out or cut it out? Well, somehow the doctor's answer did not feel right to me. My intuition was telling me there was another way! There was another option and *I was going to find it.*

Then a miracle began to happen.

Listening to Inner Guidance

I began to receive guidance, as I had as a child, from that place within. I believed it and I began to listen. But this guidance was so distinctly different from what I heard before.

It was amazing! I moved from my head space, my chattering mind, into a totally different arena.

I listen because it felt true. I had the confidence that if I followed it, I would be healed. I did not know how I was going to heal; I just knew I would heal.

We all have truth residing inside of us, and it will speak to us when we listen. It rings true for *us*. If truth is followed, it produces amazing results. I was listening, and knew I was on to something. This profound discovery of mine was triggered by the challenge of a stage-4 tumor. That is the power of turning tragedy into triumph, into advantage. I understood this was the beginning of accessing the advantage.

Note to Self: Trust and know you will receive the answers and you will.

I had turned my efforts from looking at my outer circumstances being gravely ill, to saying I am healed. I heard my inner voice respond to me as I reached out for Life.

Life responded to me and I listened, I was very still. I heard my inner voice speak softly and sweetly to me. I became more aware of my surroundings. My inner voice spoke and said: *"Look at how you feel about everything around you. Being aware brings healing. Being aware brings life."* This Divine Healer within is the connection to our Source. I discovered my inner healer.

To sum it up, it is 'The Great I AM presence that is in All.'

There was a victorious, conquering feeling that came over me that allowed me to rise up and embrace life. I was transforming the physically challenged me into someone and something much stronger.

My Increased Awareness is My Healing

One thing that the sickness did was place me in a situation of being still; so still, that all I could do was think and breathe.

I was able to review my life and take inventory of what I had become. I began to think about life and the mystery of it all. I started to think about all the times in my life when I had the opportunity to do something I really wanted and I put it off, saying, "I'm young, I got plenty of time! I will do it tomorrow." At this point of my life I was not sure if tomorrow would ever come. I knew that the only thing I really had was the opportunity of being in the here and now!

Time constantly changes; it is an illusion. Time is fleeting. It is a great misconception to think we have all the time to do something when-time is never promised. If you really wish to do something, do not be deceived into thinking you have time to put it off. Do it now! For *now* is all we have.

Increased Awareness

Learning to increase my awareness was a valuable step forward in my healing process. If you are faced with health issues or similar challenges, I suggest you consider these simple awareness tools that I put to work in my own life.

Increased awareness is being aware of the thoughts, feelings and action that were around three years prior to your illness. Ask yourself, "What major events were occurring at the time?" Begin to go back in time to search out the root cause of your illness. Write down any feelings, thoughts, events and actions that may have triggered your illness. This awareness brings healing. The healing occurs by eliminating the thought forms that created the illness in the first place.

The thoughts and feelings will be discussed later on in this book. You will learn what emotions, thoughts and feelings affect which organs. This information is based on two thousand years of medical practice in China.

Ask yourself how did I create this illness?

Once you know how you created it, you then have the power to UN-create it.

Note to Self: Life carries with it wonderful challenges, so face them, look at them, and accept them. These Challenges become the gems of life that allow you to express a life worth having. Give yourself permission to have it now.

Chapter 4:

Life Connection

As I began to evaluate my life and health challenges, I noticed I was holding anger. I was carrying a lot of childhood pain.

Pain and Negative Emotions

Emotionally, I had resentment. I wanted to blame someone else for my plight, my unhappiness. I recalled being a very sensitive child. My feelings got hurt very easily. I was always worrying about something. Little I did know or understand that negative emotions turned on me in the form of disease. My cells were being bathed with these negative emotions, and this ultimately created the conditions for cancer.

I never knew or understood that cells mutate according to thoughts and emotions. I will explain this more in detail later in this book. My seething anger turned into deep resentment. That resentment festered in my cells until the normal function of those cells became disrupted and cancerous.

I had to come to understand the strong relationship between my emotions and disease. My true healing began once I gained awareness and insight into my sickness.

Releasing the Blame

I released the blame and used the balm of forgiveness for myself and others. I found the lightness inside of me by taking away the heavy significance of circumstances that happened to me. As I did this, my body began to heal. I call the heaviness, *density*. More on density, and what it is, in my next book called *"Density."* I found density is directly correlated to emotional issues that may spur on certain disease processes.

I believe all illness presents itself into our lives to help us gain better clarity on who and what we are. Once embraced, it shows our true human potential and capacity to heal ourselves. Later in this very book is a guide that tells which emotions lead to wellness and which ones do not.

Let's get in the habit of honoring the spark and joy of living by speaking-"I am well, and it is so." *Life and death is truly in the power of our speaking.*

Following Inner Instructions

As I listened within, I was told specific things to kick start my healing. The first thing my inner voice guided me to do was get fresh flowers in my hospital room and look at, and appreciate, the flowers.

Roses were my favorite. I loved the fresh aroma of roses. It was aromatically hypnotic. It made me feel better once I inhaled and felt the aroma of roses. I was guided to observe how beautiful they were. I looked at the flowers often. Observing the beautiful shape and color took my mind off of being sick. I saw myself well, whole, and complete like the flower. I felt like I was absorbing the beautiful essence of the flower into my very being.

The next instruction was to drink lots of pure water. I purchased bottled spring mineral water. I imagined it flushing the toxins and sick cells out of my body. I started feeling so much better that the doctor was pleasantly surprised. I was soon released from the hospital.

Next, I was led to go out of doors, into the sunshine and sunbathe for fifteen minutes a day. As I felt the warmth of the sun's rays, I imagined the sun purifying me and burning all the impurities and cancerous cells out of my body.

The greatest shift in my healing, however, was learning to forgive myself and others. I had to just let all that past stuff go! Holding on to past hurts and resentments was not serving me. It only made me feel worse.

Whew! Breathe! I learned not to take everything so personally.

Embracing My Purpose

In hindsight, I further embraced my friend's

encouraging words that day, *I will live!* Along with the prayers of Skipper and Mindy, something profound shifted within me. Energy began to pour into my body and my thoughts that encouraged me to bring forth my true purpose for living. I determined to live more profoundly and more meaningfully as the being that I am.

Note to Self: Before I could receive healing I had to believe it was possible. All healing is possible to those who believe.

Of course, healing and finding one's true purpose in life is a process. With my choice to live, life began that day for me in the hospital. I shifted from a dying mentality to wanting to live and live the best life possible! I began to believe that I deserved a beautiful life.

Time to Follow my Inner Voice

I followed my inner voice's instructions; it led me to my healing and transformation. By listening to my still small voice, it has led me to who and what I am today – *whole*. But, I am moving ahead of the story.

I want to emphasize that transformation began when I first accepted that I was sick, and responsible for creating my sickness. Then I believed I deserved to live. Next, I began to question and seek answers.

And then, most profoundly, I began to listen. As I followed instructions I was led on a fantastic journey called *my life*.

If I would have been home at 5 p.m. that day, watching the evening news, I would not have had this amazing life transformation! Life began to turn around just like when night turns into day.

I discovered this great power to live. This great power is within each and every one of us. My purpose in life began to unfurl. As I questioned the things about life, I wanted to know how and why I got sick. The answers came one by one.

I discovered that:

In my deepest despair there was hope.

I started to breathe deeply; in my breath

there was life.

I began to listen to my inner voice.

My inner self began to talk to me.

In the silence, I found a friend.

The great friend was within.

Yes, truly, a good friend is like medicine!

That medicine brought health to my soul.

This book is an account of the dynamic shift of my consciousness from sickness to health. I am so truly grateful that I came to understand that process; and so grateful that I began to listen to the guiding voice from within.

As I listened, the answers became evermore clear, crystal clear.

My questions were being answered:

Note to Self: When things don't go my way, do not automatically think you know why and make up negative stories about it. Ask "What else could this mean?" Create a positive story about it. Generate happy meanings, and so shall happiness follow the meanings.

Chapter 5:

On the Road Called *Life*

Upon release from the hospital, I was faced with receiving six months of chemotherapy, I did not know what to do. I began to feel afraid and uncertain.

I had known people who had chemotherapy and it did not turn out so well for them. I saw their hair fall out, and I observed them wither away like a dried leaf on a tree until they succumbed to the cancer illness. *Would this be my fate? A dwindling down to nothingness, will I be taken down from the cancer or the chemo?* My mind raced with possibilities. None of the possibilities that I thought of seemed to be a viable option. I asked the doctor *again,* just to make sure I did not miss anything.

"Doc, are you sure there isn't anything I can do to heal this disease?" The doctor looked at me sternly and said, "I am sorry but no, there is not a cure for cancer."

"So why have chemo?" I responded.

"It is the recommended treatment for stopping the spread of the disease inside your body." He calmly explained.

The question I ask myself is: "Do I embark on a six month journey down the rabbit hole, not knowing where I will land?" I felt inside that there is some other way to heal the disease than what the doctor was explaining to me. It was a strong gut feeling.

The Chemo Experience

I came to the conclusion six months is not that long to stop the disease process. Yet, I went the path of following my Doctor's advice of getting chemotherapy. I did not know at the time what else to do. As I expected, the chemo side effects were devastating on my body.

I felt sick unto death. But, I patiently completed the six months program as recommended by my doctor. I was thrilled with expectancy that the disease was contained. Now perhaps I could be done with this illness once and for all.

Yet, after six months of chemotherapy the Doctor wanted me to have another operation and more chemo. I was upset over this, thinking why couldn't he have handled everything the first time? Now he wanted to cut my body open again? I could not face the turmoil of suffering. I sought that eternal part of me and said "I'd rather leave this earth than be experiencing that again."

I was so distraught I called a family member on the phone about this. She had been a nurse for over thirty years. I call her Grandma Griffin.

Grandma Griffin said, "No one ever told me you were that sick and in the hospital. I would have visited you."

This wonderful Grandma had made a point of adopting kids who needed mothering in the neighborhood. She had even raised all of her kids' kids and the grandkid's kids! After I told her my whole grim sickness story, she was surprised, "Why didn't anyone tell me you were sick and in the hospital?" Grandma asked me again, to make certain I would not to let that happen again. She wanted to be kept in the loop.

"I felt you had enough stuff to worry about, Grandma Griffin."

"You let me decide that!" she said.

"Did the doctor tell you about the Ca125 blood test?" Grandma Continued on.

"What is that?" I was thinking what else I now have to be bothered with?

After going through the long exhaustive hospitalization and chemotherapy, I was worn out. I felt overwhelmed to learn about more procedures.

"It is a blood test that indicates the presence of ovarian cancer," Grandma said. This was in 1991 and Grandma Griffin knew about this test.

"No, my doctor never mentioned it." I began thinking what else did my Doctor not tell me?

"Well ask about it, and if it is negative, there is a chance you won't need surgery," Grandma Griffin said. I heard the surprise in her voice. "Did he recommend for you to get a sonogram after the first surgery instead of wanting to cut you open again?"

"Nope, he never said anything about it," I replied. Wow, isn't this something?

I was surprised at the Doctor not fully explaining all of my options, but there could have been a chance my doctor did not know about what Grandma Griffin was suggesting.

I realized that just because a person is a medical doctor does not mean that person has all the knowledge there is to know about the body. I assumed that doctors are supposed to know, but they are all human. And all humans have limited knowledge.

I had a personal awakening that helped me to realize that the source within me knows all. I would be led by that.

Right then and there I made up my mind. I would not give anyone power over my life in making decisions for my body anymore. I would take charge of my health from that day by being proactive. I would take charge by searching for the information I needed to heal my own body. Knowing that my body was invaded by blades, knives, and titanium staples, made me feel like my body did not fully belonged to me anymore. I would begin the journey of reclaiming my body again. I would have much preferred a non-invasive blood test. Besides, that would have been a much simpler procedure. It is true that what you do not know can dynamically affect your life.

Note to Self: You are in control of your body, and mind. Be accountable for all choices you make about your mind and body. This leads to a happy soul.

"Well, now, you listen to me, okay?" Grandma said in a stern voice.

52

"Okay I will," I responded intently.

"You get yourself another Doctor, and I mean right away!"

"You find yourself someone who knows about the tests I just told you about and will do them first before suggesting surgery. Do you understand?"

"Yes, I will." I replied quickly, for I felt the seriousness of her tone.

"Okay, now you call me if you have any more problems; and know I am praying for you. Keep in touch and call somebody every now and then!" She said bye to me and hung up the phone.

I knew I would follow her advice. I would put off having the second operation and find another doctor. The decision felt right.

Transformation

My old doctor wrote me warning letters stating if I did not return for another operation, I was putting my life in danger. I didn't respond.

After searching and following my own inner voice and research, I found a holistic medical doctor. I worked with him closely and followed his advice about exercise, along with natural hormone replacement and intravenous vitamin therapies.

As I embraced life, I began to search for all the ways to extend my life. I knew that knowledge and understanding are keys for transformation. I wanted to learn about all the different healing paths. I eagerly began to learn how to heal naturally.

I began to study all types of ways to balance the body, and my body was responding.

I really believe that my body began to heal because I *believed* it would. *All things are possible when one believes!*

There are scientific studies proving this is so. It is called *epigenesist,* the study that our DNA is affected by what we think, more so than genetics.

I began to study natural and alternative therapies, like herbal medicine and crystal gemstone therapy. I learned about the chakra system. I began to study Chinese medicine and acupressure therapies. I learned Reiki, reflexology and iridology. I began to study natural skin care. I studied chelation therapies, meditation and vegetarian diets. I also studied vitamin, nutritional and enzyme therapies.

I began to expand and explore anything I could get my hands on that I thought would extend and heal my life.

Since I now realized life is a gift, I was determined to be healed. I was fortunate to gather such wonderful information. The more I learned, the more I wanted to know. I embraced my life; I was determined never to allow the disease of cancer to reign in my life again.

By practicing healthy living and believing, I felt my body become stronger. I changed how I thought. I changed my conversation about my illness. I changed what I ate. The body has to use more energy to break down processed foods and heavy meats. I needed all my resources and energy to rebuild my body. The less energy I used to digest processed foods and heavy meats, the easier it was for my body to rebuild and heal.

I became a vegetarian and I took several natural supplements. I drank liquids, more water, fruit and vegetable juices.

I started to exercise on a regular basis.

I got wiser and stronger. I began to wear quartz crystals. Crystals infuses the body with energy. Most watches keep time by quartz crystals.

I was on a routine plan of meditation, exercise and stretching. Coming so close to dying shook my very foundation. I would have tried anything feasible to get my health back. I never once went back to the previous doctor who sent me those scary warning letters wanting me to have more surgery. He stated in his letters that I going against medical advice. The letter sounded as if I had broken the law or something. If it didn't work the first time, what was the proof it would work the second time around? I think back and laugh about it now, especially because my following a different course proved I did not need surgery. I am truly healed without it!

Note to Self: When something does not feel right down in your gut, more than likely it isn't!

I chose another route that felt right to me. I am so thankful that I did. I am very much grateful for Grandma Griffin who gave me the heads-up about alternatives other than surgery.

I am amazed of the knowledge and strength of my wise elders. Folks like my Seminole Grandma Leila and Grandma Sylvia Griffin, helped shape my life and impacted me in a profound way. They are my heroes. I have gained much knowledge by listening to the wisdom of my elders.

Thanks to Source Energy and my inner guidance system, I became totally healed, stronger and healthier. I discovered there are other ways of healing besides conventional, western medicine. I do have considerable respect for western medicine, but there are other healing modalities that are just as effective or more so.

I always investigate everything, so I can then make an informed decision. I am so happy that I followed my inner guidance that day. I began to connect with like-minded seekers to discover how to heal myself. I knew I had to be pro-active and vigorous in finding the answers. It was my intention to live and to heal. I needed a clear map on how to do that. That map began by going within.

Like lighting candles one at a time, healing is possible one person at a time. My light was turning on for healing. I felt so alive!

A New World

This new world I found was within me.

I discovering this world for myself for the first time. But this world was there all along.

I was in times past looking at life from an external reference only, and I now turned inward. Life before was from what I could physically see and what I could deduce from external observation. This was an intellectual, analytical, factual, material and visible ego world. To truly know *life* is to understand and observe the things that are of wisdom, both subtle and unseen. I always wanted to know the truth. I always wanted to be led by the truth and I was a seeker.

Have you ever known and felt there's more to life? Have you ever wanted to seek what life is truly about?

If you said *yes*, then you are like me. I was looking for eternal bliss, wanting relief, peace, and joy. But yet, I knew that something was missing in my life, and I was not quite figuring out what that was.

My self-discovery did not happen overnight but it did happen. It was truly a wonderful enfoldment, like flower petals blooming, not all at once but more like one at a time. For me, as I continued to open up to greater discovery, it was about being receptive to my inner guidance system. Life continued to demonstrate to me more possibilities of being fully alive.

I found the pain and suffering that I had endured from the sickness worked in my favor in the over-all picture of life. It drove me within to that subtle, unseen world. It led me to know Source Energy.

To me it is what people called God. If examined deeply, illness can be the inner healer of your Soul asking you to look at your life in a different way.

The Higher Life Source is asking for a more direct connection to our intuition.

Connecting to Source

When I speak of 'Source Energy' I am speaking of the Source of everything and everyone. I will not put a name on it because it is known by different cultures by different names, but when I studied it, I got that everyone is speaking and trying to describe aspects of the same thing. I believe it is that which is indescribable, that which is unseen, and the life force that connects all of us.

At the time, my outer world was full of doubts and concerns. Inside my imagination, inside my inner world, I could be healthy, brilliant and in touch with my inner-self. My imagination became my playground. It was there I began to convince myself of the possibilities that are available for me and my life. It was and still is an unfolding process.

That process lead to me to the true healing power within. In my weakest time, I became strong

The process of going 'within,' what did it mean? This process of going within was composed of my emotions, my gut feelings, visualizations, inner prayers, and meditations. Also, it was a trusting and courageous process. I could not go anywhere, my body was restricted. Being restricted in my outer world gave me unlimited freedom in my inner world. That restriction was good for me because it opened me up to other possibilities in my world. I began to listen to my inner guidance system.

I was looking for answers because I was uncomfortable in my physical body. I began to receive answers and sobering thoughts. I began to follow these thoughts and they led me to examine this wonderful machine called the body. The body will show you and tell you everything it needs to stay in balance. What I discovered was amazing!

Now, I am clear that it does not matter what happened to me as a child or what happened in my relationships. I was the one interpreting my life's circumstances and making it mean whatever I was making it mean. I do not say this to make light or diminish what happened, but to re-contextualize what happened so it empowers me rather than disempowered me.

I discovered this new world by identifying the power of breathing and listening to my inner voice; by respecting and honoring this life force that flows in and out. What can ever be accomplished without the breath? Being mindful and aware of its presence leads us to the ever unfolding development of our lives. It puts life into a more simple perspective.

Note to self: Life has simple answers if I am willing to listen.

The Healing Law of Attraction

I have shared my information with thousands of people throughout the years. It can start by you sharing this book with others to get the word out that you are in charge of your life.

Now through sharing this book, we can go to tens of thousands.

What you are looking for is also looking for you.

This great mind, spirit, and body of ours is truly amazing! Look into your thoughts – this one the first principles of all your creations. I stated *"I AM HEALED,"* and it actually translated into reality in my body. There is a science that actually proves what

I am saying. Scientists are finally catching up to what the ancient ancestors knew all along. They knew and understood that what we say – if we *believe* in what we say – we can create it and manifest it in our bodies and in our physical world. Hence, all things are possible to him that believes. Epigenetics is the study of how stress and diet releases bio-chemicals in the body that affect the DNA, an important factor of influence on our health and body's life span.

Also quantum physics- shows how the mind interacts with our beliefs, affecting how humans view the world. Check out 'What the Bleep Do We Know?' It is a documentary film that explains what we see from what we do not see. This world is more than what we physically see. Quantum physics have proven it from a scientific stand-point.

I had the chance to work with the first holistic medicine practice in New York, where I expanded my knowledge and assisted many others from all over the world to balance their lives and improve their health. All healing begins with one fundamental thing – desire!

After desire comes the action. I began to do what my inner voice led to me to do. The juicing, the fasting, the praying the mediation, the re-educating myself of true healing practices.

All disease is an opportunity to change the old pattern and ways of existence to embrace life on a higher dimension.

Once I had the desire to live by faith and my inner leading, I was lead to the knowledge of improving health. The Law of Attraction says in essence, that *what you think about and believe you attract into your life*. We attract everything into our lives by virtue of what thoughts we hold in our mind. I had to take responsibility, I attracted the disease, and I also changed my thoughts and I attracted the healing. The answers are always there if one listens. Attraction means nothing without action.

Embrace this wonderful journey called life. Face it fully and create it to be what you want it to be.

If you were driving down the wrong road and you realized it, you would turn around and go down the road of your intended destination. Life's roads are something like that. I also see life like a piece of marble in which we are constantly carving out and chiseling rock to create a beautiful sculpture! It takes vision and action.

I wish to share with you what I learned. I hope it will encourage you to embrace life to the fullest.

Note to Self: Life is truly what you make it.

Seeing Is Believing

From all of my life changing experiences, inquiries and studies, I embarked on some amazing stuff about the body, mind and the universe! It totally revolutionized my thinking and way of being.

There is more to life than what meets the eye. There is more to life than what the ears hear. I was born with very poor eyesight. I felt like I came out of the womb needing glasses!

The first thing I used to do as soon as I woke up was reach for my glasses. Without them, I couldn't see *nada,* nothing! When I put on my glasses everything was crystal clear!

The unseen realm is like that! The naked eye has a hard time perceiving.

That unseen realm is right here with us, but without spiritual glasses we are unable to see it or perceive it. One day my life opened up to other realms. It was incredible. I will share that story in a later chapter.

The unseen realm is in each and every one of us. It is like turning on the light switch and being able to see something we were unable to see before because we were in darkness.

Mankind could not see germs until the microscope was invented. The microscope opened up a whole world of germs. Before quantum physics was discovered, scientist thought the atom was the smallest particle. Now, quantum physics have subatomic, quantum and quark particles smaller than the atom. I believe there are even smaller particles yet to be discovered. The unseen realm is similar, in that one needs spiritual perception to see into the unseen world. After looking deeper into this life, it is possible to discover this fantastic world.

Ok, my belief system changed from being religious to spiritual. I had changed my religious practices and dogmas to studying and understanding nature. GOD also, for me, stood for the *Great Out Doors.* In nature there is divine intelligence. In observing nature I discovered and learned about Divine Intelligence. There is a purpose for everything and in observing nature I could see intricate patterns about life.

All my laws and principles are based in that truth. Not in the traditions of men. I learned to let go of what society said God was, and I began to study what 'Divine Source Intelligence' is. That intelligence is in every soul. All one has to do is seek it and access it. It is always there like a beacon in the night, shinning the light to the path of truth.

One thing was for sure, all of religion and my belief in the Supreme Being did not stop me from getting sick. There are a lot of religious and spiritual people who are experiencing sickness. To me sickness was not in my plan. There was more knowledge I needed to have to prevent sickness. It is stated: seek and you will find. Life is a continuous seeking of truth. I am committed to never stop looking and questioning. That is humility at the soul level. Never think you know it all. I learned that the more I think I know, the more life shows me, I don't

The beauty is to allow life to contribute to me, as I am the sum of the contribution.

Life Force Energy

Stay open to the truth and it will reveal itself to you. It is important to identify and release all fear!

By connecting to the unseen, we can connect to the power of the life force. Some call it *Chi* energy, some call it *Qi*. This life force or Chi energy flows on the earth and inside our bodies. When our Chi energy is blocked, disease ensues. It is tied in deeply with our belief system and our emotions.

The Chinese have known about this unseen energy flowing through the body and Earth for at least

5000 years. The Acupuncture System is built on the Chi energy system. It is vital to keep the life force flowing for optimum health and healing of mind, body and spirit.

In my healing phase, I received acupuncture and healing energy touch therapies to assist with my energy. I also began to learn more about the Chi force and how it connects with our body's health. From my experience, I found Chinese medicine very helpful. It was very knowledgeable of how emotions affect the body. In comparison, allopathic (western medicine) has been around less than 250 years.

The study of Chinese medicine confirms extensive research and documentation in comparison to the effects of western medicine. Acupuncture does not have the serious side effects of western medicine. The needles are usually not painful. Other modalities that work with Chi force that are conducive to healing and maintenance of well-being are Chi-Gong, Chi-Kung, Reiki, energy balancing, crystal therapies, chakra balancing, reflexology and iridology. Please see the book list to familiarize yourself with these helpful modalities. These are time-tested, effective healing practices that have worked for me and many others. The more we understand about alternative healing modalities, the more options we will have for healing.

I have witnessed peoples' lives changing and healing for the better using a blend of different treatments. I personally have had a very high success rate in balancing people's lives, and in teaching them how to take better care of their bodies.

Do not be afraid of the unseen. Acknowledge it

and be in harmony with it. It has wonderful and effective teachings and wisdom within its embrace.

Note to Self: Be courageous and embrace your fears to master the Self.

Experiencing Abundant Life!

These unseen forces guide us in our life. We are meant to live life more abundantly. We are made to experience joy and happiness; our bodies were designed to experience fullness of joy.

Every organ in our body vibrates to a specific frequency that is in tune with our 'happy and joy-joy' responses to life. Every organ resonates to a sound. There are heartfelt *buttons* that reside within us, and when activated they allow for greater capacity for a healthy life. It is felt as an expansion in our energy field; meaning, when you have these thoughts you feel good, you feel open and expansive. You have creative and happy thoughts. Our immune system, our circulation, and our reproductive and creativity, all respond to our boost of happy and joy responses.

When the body responds in disharmony for a period of time *dis-ease* follows. It actually takes an average three minutes of continuous thought for that particular thought to become a part of our physical structure. Depending on the nature of the disharmonious thoughts and feelings, a particular disease is invoked. It causes a particular pattern. I like to call it energy, and as energy is felt it becomes vibrations.

The type of vibrations that I am speaking of is generated within and is felt without, using energy

65

from the 'etheric world' or 'unseen world' and became manifest in the physical world. Imagine our bodies as transmitters able to receive and send frequencies. These frequencies can create wellness or sickness. That is how thoughts can actually cause physical illness.

I began my healing the day I began thinking and saying *I am healed.* Today I no longer experience that particular sickness! I am very grateful to all my relations, ancestors and the great Divine Infinite Creator of the Universe for my clear direction. My message is this: If you desire something strongly enough you will be given direction and information on how to get it. Once you get the information, then it is time to put it into action. If you want it ask for it; receive it and you can have it. It sounds simple and it is.

Note to self: The breath brings positive change. It brings power to change my life. Breathe consciously to access the deeper levels of myself.

Chapter 6:

Life's Secret Helpers

I have a secret that will absolutely heal every ailment and get you through every single challenge you will have in life. Want to know what it is?

Life has secret helpers that few understand.

Let's start with the breath. Everything is accomplished by this one act...*Breathing!*

Your breath is unique and it is a gift from the unseen realm. None of us can create it. It comes from a place you have never seen. Think about that! Give honor to this place. Knowing it will regenerate you. Keep breathing, for everything is accessed by the breath. In some cultures the breath and spirit means the same thing. The breath is what keeps us alive. We need it more than water, more than food, it is the life force.

I learned in Native American cultures, they access the inner world by changing their breathing patterns and listening to drum beats that mimic the heart. In India, they have certain breathing patterns to assist them to go deeper into meditations.

In China, they started the practice Tai Chi and Chi Gong to access their inner self by slow breathing and rhythmic movements. A study from Harvard University-*Harvard Health Publications May 2009 states* Tai Chi and Qi Gong have been proven to reduce blood pressure and other health problems like Arthritis, Heart Disease and Sleep Problems. These movements and breathing have been proven to heal the body in others ways too. Persons with Parkinson's disease, Breast cancer and stroke have received positive benefits by practicing Tai Chi.

Breathe in and be kind to yourself. Breathing is another way of accepting life into your body. Breathing is a way of being present to your NOW circumstances. Breathe in the present situation and convert the energy as you breathe out, energize the present situation with your now unconditional acceptance of where you are and what is occurring in your situation.

The more you relax the more things flow. This is all accomplished to be effective in the third dimensional plane. It is so we can behold consciousness, to have and experience LIFE and have it more abundantly and experience it more profoundly.

This ability is accomplished through our vibration and our harmonics to three things: our connection to Source Energy, our connection to ourselves (internal world) and our connection to our external environment. How do we energize the breath? We energize each breath and stamp it with our own unique purpose with our thoughts! Every thought that you think creates a bio-chemical reaction in the body. These chemicals are released throughout the body and cause a reaction.

In listening to Anthony Robbins, he suggests that when we awake every morning saying I love my life with four breaths in, and four breaths out. Try it. See if you feel different, more energized and alive. I know I do. What is important for you is what you observe. That is the true marker for you. You are always breathing. Breathing is managed by your involuntary nervous system.

You continue to breathe whether you think about breathing or not, you are still breathing. You do not need to think about breathing. Thank goodness for that, for I might have forgotten to breathe a few times and I would have knocked myself out! Somewhere near the bread isle trying to figure out if I should get the raisin bread or rye. 'Bamm,' I would have forgotten to take my next breath! Next you would have heard a call for cleanup in isle 3!

We were created with such wisdom. That small but major little detail, you and I do not have worry about! The Creator took care of that for us. Complicated as life can get sometimes, that is one less complication. Isn't' that something to be grateful for?

Deep breathing, however, is conscious breathing. It is thinking about breathing; it is mindful breathing. It is written in the Bible *"The Creator breathed into man and man became a living soul."* A living soul came after God breathed into man. Connecting to ones soul through the breath is important. What are you breathing into your thoughts? What are you bringing to life?

It is in your life and it is in all life. Again, it is the All in All. It is ever present everywhere.

Powerful Inner Messengers

Each thought that you think creates a bio-chemical reaction in the body. These bio-chemicals have the ability to communicate with each cell the nature of that thought. These bio-chemicals are triggered and released by a thought. The bio-chemicals then bathe the brain and body cells. They affect each cell's behavior. They bathe the organs with their bio-chemical ingredients, to allow the body to feel your thoughts.

They are our inner messengers. For an example, if one has peaceful thoughts, those are transmitted via the bio- chemicals through the blood to each and every cell of the body to create an internal condition where peace is felt. By our inner bio-chemical messengers, the thought moves from being just a thought to now becoming a feeling. When peaceful thoughts are maintained for an average of three minutes or more, they become a physical manifestation in the body. This process can be perceived as the beginning of health or disease creation. It begins in the unseen realm first, then it manifests in that which is seen as a progression.

The key to healing is to trace the 'dis-eased' process to the thought that triggered it in the first place. Once awareness locates the start of the discomfort, healing begins. When thoughts are mixed with strong emotions, the stronger the bio-chemicals released in the body. The body perceives every emotion through these bio-chemicals. These bio-chemical thoughts have vibrations that are measured as brain-wave activity. They are produced by the body and are hormonal and chemical transmitters that actually regulate the entire body.

As you think and feel what you are thinking, thoughts are experienced by the body as hormones and bio-chemicals. These bio-chemicals are released into the blood stream. We control theses bio-chemicals by changing our thoughts. Think *I am healed. I am happy. I love my life. I am grateful for life. I say yes to life.* As you say it and feel it- your biochemical makeup changes and so does your health.

In the book by author Robert Thayer called *"Calm Energy: How People Regulate Mood with Food and Exercise,"* he presents his view that optimal mood involves increased happiness, pointing out when people experience happiness they tend to have higher energy and lower tension.

Scientists have actually been able to map the part of the brain that generates happiness and the part of the brain that generates sadness. This was studied at the *Laboratory for Affective Neuroscience* at the University of Wisconsin. In 2004 at Bowling Green State University in Ohio, scientists used MRI to read the reactions of people when they simply imagined emotions. When subjects imagined laughter, the left side of their brain's *"happiness"* circuits were stimulated and they reported a reduction in sadness. Sadness or negative emotions were linked to the right side of the brain when they imagined being sad.

Positive emotions are linked to happiness. Negative emotions are linked to sadness.

Happiness is felt and manufactured by our hormones and bio-chemicals that are released into the body. Your body begins to actually feel happiness.

Begin to hold a happiness thought for three minutes; it will become a part of your physical being. Why three minutes? It takes an average of three minutes for each cell or bio-chemical to circulate throughout the entire body.

Happiness Medicine Exercise:

Think of something wonderful and something happy right now. Imagine that all of your round little cells have smiley faces on them. These smiley faces are now circulating around in your blood system. These little round smiley cells are now assisting your body to be happy and healthy.

Now hold this feeling for 3 minutes.

After holding this thought and feeling for three minutes:

How do you feel?

Do you feel happier?

"Thoughts become things and thoughts can become words; words shape and create our world!" SaEnya

---

As I Think, I Create

As I reflected back on the cancer, I understood how the pathway was created for its existence in my life. I also discovered how to reverse it.

I passed the five year mark with no reoccurrence. Then came the ten year mark, then the fifteen year mark, then the twenty year mark and no more cancer! What a celebration!

Not only did I believe it, time also had proven that I not only reversed the disease, but I am cured! I had the opportunity to examine and talk with other people who had developed cancer as well. I discovered an interesting connection. To understand how something is created will allow one the understanding to heal it.

By understanding and knowing our body's function, we become conscious of who and what we are. We can then choose to live consciously in everything that we think and do. By thinking happy thoughts, we release our own natural medicine. There was a man whose disease and pain was subsided through laughter his name was Norman Cousins, he wrote a book called, *"Anatomy of an Illness."*

Electrical, Energetic, Magnetic, Vibrational

We are more than physical beings, we are emotional, mental, magnetic, electrical and most of all vibrational. Vibrational means, we have an inner guidance system that communicates with us through our feelings, moods and energy levels. The heart beats, the stomach churns, the lungs make sounds through air flowing in and out, the kidneys filter and stream fluid, the blood flows to a particular rate and makes sound.

When a practitioner is listening to the heart and lungs with a stethoscope, it is to hear theses sounds, rates and rhythms. If any of these rates accelerate or decelerate outside the normal rhythm; disease or death can result. There are studies demonstrating how listening to certain meditative sound frequencies can heal the mind and emotions.

Meditation

Bi-neural beats, discovered by Heinrich W. Dove in 1839, showed that certain sounds at two different pitches induced relaxation and healing. The emotions are the control seat of the body. The emotions are the gateway to health and healing. Meditation practiced regularly and effectively will balance the emotions and mind.

I also learned to meditate after learning how to connect with my breath. There are thousands of studies showing the benefits of mediation. Meditating for only fifteen to twenty minutes twice per day brings enormous health benefits like reducing strokes, blood pressure, stress, anxiety, pain, depression and insomnia. It has decreased cholesterol, reduced congestive heart failure, increased intelligence and improved personality traits.

Studies also showed increased productivity, reversal of aging and reduced conflict.

Cortisol *(a hormone that can cause aging)* levels drop when the body is in meditation; this also increases growth hormones (anti-aging hormones). Having a body in perfect harmony is one of my definitions of balanced health.

The Power of the Breath

The breath is a nutrient that the body, mind and the Great Spirit (Source Energy) uses to navigate through this world. No one knows where it comes from or where it goes. It directs the quality of our lives. A continuous flow of the breath that is focused on the beautiful, joyful and blissful pleasures of life creates an attraction and magnetism for all good things.

The ancients knew that the secret to mastering thoughts was through the breath. The breath controls the thought. There are different levels of vibrational thoughts. Thinking along these various levels produce certain types of reactions and can lead your life towards either sickness or health.

The Amazing Body

Form determines function. To understand how something is formed will give insight to its function. There is a divine intelligence to everything created. Behind divine intelligence is divine thought.

I am very amazed at how each body acts so brilliantly! It manufactures its own medicine. It actually heals itself when placed in the right conditions. This complex machine is wonderfully made.

It took nine months for your body – your living temple – to form in your mother's womb. Your heart pumps anywhere between 1,500 to 2,000 gallons of blood per day; that is 547,500 to 730,000 gallons per year! Your body takes in an average 15-18 breaths per minute, without any conscious thoughts about the heart beating or the breath breathing. The body is made up of 206 bones, 50-75 trillion cells, 3 billion nerves; 300 million nerves are in the brain alone.

The body has the capacity to take what you eat and convert it into fuel for energy for you to perform optimally. The body is comprised of systems that regulate our mental and emotional intelligence. The body is like a receiving and transmitting channel or portal for your thoughts and vibrations.

The body is made perfectly to do and accomplish great things. It interacts perfectly with outside elements. It generates heat to keep you warm, and has a cooling system to keep you cool. The danger comes when the body is not appreciated. This fine machine took Divine Intelligence and great detail to create. It takes a tremendous amount of orchestration to have the basic functions of the body operate correctly.

Sickness is a sign that the body and mind's natural laws were broken or misunderstood. Mistreating or ignoring the body is like owning a *Maserati* sports car and treating it like a two wheel bicycle. With mind and body we have an emotional, spiritual and mental connection and guidance system to create wonderful things in life. This all occurs so we can think and move and have our being in this third dimensional plane – our world. It is so we can behold consciousness; to have LIFE and have it more abundantly.

Understand how the body works and you understand your life! Bio-chemicals and neurotransmitters are constantly released and fired in the body. These bio-chemicals align from your thoughts. They also regulate the entire body. This allows your body to actually feel what you're thinking.

As pointed out earlier, it takes three minutes of consistent thought for that thought to actually become a part of your physical structure. This is because on a physical level, it takes an average of three minutes for a single blood cell, which has been bathed in a particular biochemical or thought, to circulate from one point and return back to that same point again. To take care of the body is to also understand the basics of how it functions. By taking proper care of the body we show appreciation for our life.

The Conscious and Unconscious Body

Most functions of the body are natural and beyond our conscious command. For, the body has its own intelligence. It has its own consciousness. Before, the days of being stricken with sickness, I was privileged to experience something truly wonderful and amazing. I was in the birthing room, preparing for the birth of my daughter.

Bright lights were shining down all around me, with about a half a dozen strangers in the room waiting for my imminent delivery. Without my consent or authority my body began to bear down and I felt a pushing sensation. I screamed out "I 'gotta' push, I 'gotta' push!"

"Not yet!" The doctor shouted. "You're not fully dilated! You will tear yourself badly if you push now! Breathe and don't pushhhhh!"

I listened but to my surprise, I was not the one pushing. My body simply took over and was actually pushing for me! As a result, I gave birth to a beautiful baby girl; though, in truth, my body gave birth.

That proved to me the body has its own intelligence outside my conscious mind. Anyone who has thrown up can tell you that. It is unpleasant it happens usually involuntarily. This shows the body has its own intelligence and it knows what is required to stay balanced. We breathe without thinking about it. Our heart beats without us having to remember or focus. There are functions that our body constantly does or produces without our conscious control.

To understand the body is wisdom for maintaining good health. The body is like a finely managed company made up of many workers. When these workers are appreciated and cared for they work harmoniously. Disease is a form of revolt from the workers, as a result of poor working conditions.

Your life's secret helpers are your body, mind and breath. Learn how to keep your body workers happy and you will have a healthy body company.

Note to self: Everyday, I understand more and more of the mysteries of the body and how to access it.

Chapter 7:

Mind Games and Wisdom

When I was a child I was happy just to be alive. As I got older I became more and more unhappy. I did not know why. I felt like a failure. I felt like no one loved me.

The Power of the Mind

When I look at my own unhappiness it always stemmed from what I was making my life mean from life's external circumstances.

I did not get that new car, so it meant I was not successful. The guy I loved cheated on me so I made it mean I was unlovable. I didn't get along with people at my job so I made it mean I was an unlikable person, a recluse, and an outcast. I was living in a frigid cold place so I made it mean I live in a drab city so I felt drab. I noticed all of people around me who were unhappy were doing the same thing I was doing. Complaining about my circumstances only made me feel worse.

However, I was the one giving meaning to everything. I was the one making it mean what it had meant.

The Wisdom of Changing Our Stories

Then it came to me; why not create a meaning that is empowering, joyful and peaceful?

If I change the story I change how I see the circumstances. That is how we humans are designed. Our thoughts manage our circumstances. Creating sickness is a circumstance; it does not happen randomly. It is a series of events that are created by vibrations. We create things to mean something because that is what creators do! We are creators! We make something mean something that more than likely has nothing to do with what really occurred.

It is what we want it to mean; it is our perception. The brain is wired that way to constantly make things mean 'stuff' that may not be reality at all. All day and night the brain is working on 'stuff.'

When actually the meaning that we make up is all within our own heads! We are the ones thinking it. My unhappiness seemed to come from not mastering the space between my two ears. I had all these meanings of what I thought life meant. Yet, I came to find that they had nothing to do with life. I determined to change a circumstance that was negative to a positive one! It is all made up anyhow! It was like being a child. In referring to children they tend to have strong, vivid imaginations. We can learn from that. It is a key to staying free and happy. Make believe your life is what you want it to be, then what you believe will have more of a chance of coming true. Marry beliefs with actions and the chance of a desire coming true has now doubled.

When I examined all the things I thought happiness meant, it did not mean happiness at all. How many times did I think if I only had more money, better looking clothes, lived in a different location, drove a better car, had a different job, or was with this certain person I would be happier? I was surprised to discover that once I got my life full of these *things*, I wasn't any happier. I was already seeking something else. Maybe I was happy for a little while. Then I was unhappy again.

Creating the Feelings

Then I finally got it! The experience always begins within. I am the one creating the feeling. I am the one feeling happy and I am the one choosing not to feel happy. External things were never meant to be my source of happiness. Only the beautiful, happy, and exuberant me, from within, has the ability to feel happiness. This was put there by virtue of who and what we truly are. It has nothing to do with the physical attributes on the outside.

Source Energy made us to find happiness within us. We only have to tap into the Source. Once we tune in and turn on our own inner happiness, we will always be happy and our lives will always be great. Make being happy a habit! Happiness brings healthiness. Like all things in life, happiness is a choice.

Being healthy is also a choice. It is one of the pursuits of the Soul to be happy in this life.

Learn to Flip and Switch it

I changed the meaning of what I was making cancer to mean, and it changed my life. I created an acronym for Cancer that empowered my perspective:

C – Change negative habits,
A – Alignment with your Higher Self,
N – Never give up the possibility for true healing,
C – Clarity of mind, body and soul,
E – Energize,
R – Regenerate.

I put all these thoughts into action for my healing. You can too!

Note to Self: The difference between flowers and weeds is perception.

Perhaps life is 10% of what happens and about 90% of what we make it mean! Cathy Game, RN, Brooklyn, NY.

Thoughts Become Things

Quantum Physics has discovered that thoughts become things! Thoughts are actually measurable through brain wave activity. The machine is called an EEG machine (*electrocephleogram* machine), and it measures thought waves and brain activity.

A thought is a live, measurable substance that is the source of our wellbeing. Observe the thoughts that flow through you each and every day. We have about 60,000 thoughts a day! These thoughts pass through us like waves on the ocean. There are categories of thoughts, based on the vibrational frequency where you allow your mind to dwell. Determine to control your thoughts. If you don't, then your thoughts will begin to control you.

Manifesting in the External

This is how thoughts become things! Thoughts manifest in three different levels: mental, emotional then physical. By the time the thought is manifest in our emotions, it has already penetrated the mental realm. These thoughts then manifest themselves in our physical reality. A thought then becomes an external manifestation.

When a thought persists, it will become a real reflection or a window in our external world. This external world is made up of all the things that you see with the physical eyes, and connect to with all your senses.

This is what is meant by: "As a man think in his heart so is he." KJV PR 23:7

Note to Self: Levels of thought, affects our level of being. To change our level of being, change the level of your thoughts!

To change our thoughts we must notice there is a level of dissatisfaction in the way we are now living. *(Notice how you feel.)*

A consistent complaint is also a sign that the inner soul is not finding joy and happiness, a precursor to finding one's destiny.

A real search for happiness, health and an elevated way of being requires an inner knowing that there is more to life than what you have been living or conditioned to believe or think. Ask yourself: *Is there a feeling that something is really missing from your life?*

There is an inner knowing that there is more to life than what you have been experiencing. You want to find it. You have been searching for it. You are ready for a change. The old way has not been working out. It is what has perhaps drawn you to read this book. Nothing happens by accident. Everything has a purpose. The Divine Creator creates everything for a purpose. When the purpose is gone, the being or 'thing' goes through transition or change.

If you are at what we would *call the cross-roads of life*, choosing a different path can lead you in an entirely new and rewarding direction.

Note to self: Just because you do not see something does not mean that it is not real.

Chapter 8:

Unseen Forces

I had another interesting shift in my life. It was a shift like the wind I had observed as a child on the bus that so changed my life and thoughts.

This new shift was another life changing experience that alerted to me to the more amazing, unseen forces that are at work in this universe. It proved to me that there is more to life than what I had thought.

My Grandmother's Funeral

My Seminole grandmother was my first healer and teacher, and she is and always will be so special to me. I love her so much. I vividly recall that very sad day in my life, when I was sitting outside at the final resting place for her body. It was during her funeral. I was sitting in a chair by her casket at the cemetery.

It was an overcast day, and I was looking up at that August summer's sky.

I knew this day would someday come. The Pastor was giving his blessings and saying kind words over my Grandma's casket. My Grandma was not there, of course, for I knew that casket held only her remains; now ready to enter the ground.

I was numb, no feelings, I could hardly focus on what the Pastor was saying. No words could have filled the deep void of my Grandmother's loss. When death comes, no one ever expects it.

A warm summer breeze began to flow through the whispering pines, the pine needles 'swayed' and 'swooshed' with every breeze. The sun began to peek out through the clouds. Now, it appeared that the breezes in the trees were sounding louder as if they were talking to each other. I listened intently to the trees as if I could understand what they were saying to one another.

I felt the soft, summer breezes flowing around me. I was not present as to when the Pastor stopped speaking. I sat there staring off into space. I saw people walking away leaving me there. It was time to go, yet I could not move. I sat there frozen in time. I wanted to stay there as long as I could.

She Took a Part of me with Her

The Pastor began to use a hoist to crank down the casket; it began to lower in the ground. This was good bye Grandma, I love you so much. She was the one who allowed me to be who I am today. What am I to do now?

A strange thought came over me as part of me

was seriously wishing I could go with her. When she left she took a part of me with her.

I continued sitting there as if I was glued to the back of the hard, unbalanced chair staring off into space. I did not want to stay here on Earth any longer. "Where ever you are, Grandma, please take me with you! Don't leave me down here on this crazy world!" I somehow muttered under my breath.

I was not ready to leave the silence I found at the cemetery. Somehow, I felt a strange comfort being there.

As I continued listening to the wind, I thought, *I wish I could see you one more time, Grandma.*

Feeling the longing to be with her was growing stronger and stronger as I stared down into the fresh, deep, dug hole. A bigger gust of wind was now blowing more, stronger than before, it snapped me out of my '*hazy-daze.*' I look around there was no one around me.

The Pastor had left and I did not realize it. I looked off towards the cemetery road where folks had their cars parked.

People were now walking towards the cemetery road in a slow trance-like walk. Perhaps they felt a comfort being at cemetery, as I did.

The car doors slamming off in the distance confirmed, that although comforting as it was being here, I did not belong here. I arose slowly, clutching my stomach. Not being fully present I forced myself to get up.

"Time to go to the car," I said out loud to myself while forcing my legs to move.

I began my slow, torturous walk in the direction of the parking area; step by step. My legs felt so heavy, as if each one weighed a ton. I didn't have my normal energy at all.

The Mystery Lady

As I looked up, I noticed a woman out of nowhere walking towards me very fast. She was barrowing towards me at a focused, hurried speed.

'Boy, she is really late for the funeral.' I thought.

As she approached closer to me her eyes were staring intently at mine.

She was dressed in what appeared old fashioned clothes from another era.

The mystery woman was clad in a long, black frock with what appeared outdated, black shoes. She also was wearing a black hat with a laced, black veil draping over part of her mocha soft colored, smooth face. I noticed she seemed about 5'4" or so.

Clothes from Another Time

I started wondering, where did she get those clothes from? Perhaps, she got them from a second hand store. You know, the stores that you can find stuff from decades ago. Her clothes looked well preserved even though they appeared from an earlier time frame.

She was carrying what look like a book in her left hand. It appeared like a bible, although I did not ask her what she was carrying. To me it had to be the bible, as it had a black leather case with a brown cross stitched on the front of it. I don't know why, but I vividly remember the detail on the bible.

To my surprise she walked right up to me! She called to me by name.

"Yes?" I replied. *How did she know my name? I thought.*

She spoke in slight southern accent very intently. "Your Grandmother wants you to know she is in heaven!"

Who was this Lady? How did she Know these Things?

I had never seen this woman before in my life, though I'm sure I didn't remember everyone my Grandma knew. I thought that perhaps she had seen me when I was a baby or something. I just could not ever recollect seeing her. I would have certainly remembered her because she was peculiar. Her choice of clothing was something memorable. Her soft voice I found comforting with her warm, smiling eyes anyone would have remembered her. Her words felt credible. I could not help but believe what she was saying to me. Although, what she was saying did take a stretch of faith-*how did she know my Grandma is in heaven?* I was fascinated by her statement. My mind began to open up. *Who is this mystery woman and where did she come from?*

I was thinking OK, before I could ask her "Who are you?"

She continued on saying, *"and she would like it very much if you got saved; Are you saved?"*

"No." I said. "I've been thinking about it

though, I have been going to church with a friend of mine," thinking of Hattie in the back of my mind.

More Messages

The mysterious lady at the cemetery was looking deep into my eyes. She continued and gave me more messages from my Grandmother in heaven.

"Well, your Grandmother would like it very much if you got saved!" she replied.

She never explained what she meant by that. Yet, I was getting a request from a nice lady, but a stranger, to get saved. I decided I would investigate what getting saved meant. In church they were talking about getting saved. I was not convinced. I never heard my Grandma talking about getting saved. I didn't fully understand what that meant. Now, here I was getting a request from a stranger to get saved.

However, I immediately gathered from her message that there is another dimension, an afterlife. I later understood there is a place that your soul goes after departing this life. Not everyone knows or believes this, but it is real. I like to blend science with spiritual matters because anything true is able to be proven sooner or later. In physics class, I later learned matter is neither created or destroyed it just changes form.

We are made up of matter so we are never destroyed, we continuously change form.

In respect to *getting saved*, I said, "Okay!" Not quite fully understanding the meaning behind the question. But I thought, *'If Grandma wants me to, I will do it to make her happy.'*

I wanted her to be proud of me. I would have done what my Grandma asked me to do, I knew she only wanted the best for me. To show her my love I already had made up my mind. It was comforting to know she was still around.

Wow, my Grandmother's in heaven! I thought. What excellent news! Which, I gathered that was Grandmother's intention by sending the lady to me. It was to let me know she is not dead and she went to a beautiful, harmonious place. I had comfort knowing she was happy. Also, I felt good to know that she was not really gone, she was in another place. "Who are you?" I asked.

"I am a close friend of your Grandmothers."
I thought, umm, trying to remember if or where I'd seen her before. I knew all of my Grandmother's friends, but I did not remember seeing her before.

"What is your name?" I asked.

She then told me her name, but was very unusual. Today, I cannot remember her beautiful name. Her name did not sound like it was from this dimension. I do remember it began with the letter "D" and it was a name I had never heard anyone use before. Her name was quite odd and different.

I determined to get my Grandmother's address book and look up the names of all her friends, so I could call her. She would be the one with the different name under the 'D' section of Grandma's telephone and address book.

I later looked and looked I never found any traces of her name anywhere!

Who would have known my life would have shifted that day standing by that tree. At that time my mother began calling me. "Com'on! It is time to go!"

Now You See Me,
Now You Don't

My mother was staring right at me and the woman's back was facing my mother. My Mom stood at the foot of the road by the limo about 50 yards or so.

"Well, I got to go now, but it is nice meeting you."

"It was nice seeing you too!"

As, I walked away, I thought, now that was odd, she said that as if she seen or met me before!

I took about three steps away from her, and she continued walking past me, going towards where I had just come from. I took about three steps, and something told me to turn around. I looked behind me and 'whoosh' she was gone! She was not there! I stopped and looked and looked all around in total surprise. I turned and looked up the street, she was not there. I looked down the street, she was not there. The mystery lady was nowhere to be seen.

I saw a few cars remaining and some were driving off, most were gone at this point, with only a few cars remaining from the funeral procession. If she walked to the road in front of me, I would have seen her passing me by to get to the few cars left on the road. There at the cemetery, were a lot of wide open areas, there was nowhere for her to go or hide, where I could not have seen her. Well, Mom had to have seen her because she was looking right at me.

As, I approached the car, I asked my Mom, "What happened to the lady I was talking to?"

"What lady?" My mother was looking at me curiously. I thought she was making a joke, although I found nothing funny about her response.

"The lady I was talking to while I was standing up by the tree. You were looking right at me." I pointed at the tree.

"What lady? You were not talking to no lady!" Mom stated defensively.

I guess I misread her mood, because she was really serious about her answer.

"Yes, I was! I was talking to her right when you called me!" I was perplexed.

"You were not talking to nobody. You were just standing up by the tree- that's why I called you. You are holding everybody up and we are ready to go!"

My Mother had a way of expressing herself that was blunt and always to the point. Sometimes, I had a hard time knowing when she was serious and when she was joking. This time, I felt strange to know she was serious!

Questioning my own Mind

Was I hallucinating or imaging I was talking to the nice lady?

My mind was in a state of confused curiosity. Did I see her? Of course I did! Why did my mother not see her? She was standing right there in plain sight! Well, I was determined to get to the bottom of it.

Meanwhile, we were in the *family car*, you know the limo family members ride in for a funeral.

It was my first time ever riding inside a big 'ol car like that. My Mom, my Uncle, my Auntie, my Brother and my little Sister were the ones in this long car. But, that was over shadowed by the somber occasion and this mysterious lady.

How could I tell them her message if my mother said I was never talking to anybody!

I started rubbing my hands together because I was anxiously wanting to fully understand what had taken place. It didn't make sense. Was I losing it? Was I hallucinating? Where did she go? People don't just vanish into thin air. Or maybe they do? That was certainly what seemed to have happened.

The mood in the limo was heavy and somber. I knew it was best to keep quiet when adults were quiet. I stayed out of a lot of trouble that way. The curiosity was getting the best of me. Hmm, I was really puzzled, and now thinking to ask my Uncle, perhaps he saw her. I had to get to the bottom of this mystery lady disappearance.

I blurted out, disturbing the sad atmosphere-like a lightning bolt. "Uncle, did you see me talking with a lady a little while ago by the tree?"

He was in a deep mood. I felt like his mind was somewhere else. I got that he was still in shock like we all were over Grandma's passing. He only shook his head, no!

Everybody in the car was silent. I was thinking, "This is a serious situation! Here I am, having a whole conversation with a stranger that nobody saw!"

My Aunt was overhearing the conversation with my Uncle,

"Auntie, did you see her?" Now my Auntie always spoke in a slow, quiet manner.

"No, I did not see her." She replied with her calm, sweet voice. Auntie always seemed to have a calm demeanor.

She was the kind of person you would like to talk to during an emergency situation. I could hear her now, speaking in a calm, slow voice. If there was ever a bomb threat, Auntie would have responded like "Okay, everybody there's a bomb in the building take your time exiting so no one gets hurt."

My Mom and Auntie are very beautiful women. Although they looked very much alike, they spoke very differently. My Mom spoke very fast and blunt with a deep voice. She would prank call her friends sometimes and pretend that she was a man. They would often fall for it.

The car now was more unusually quiet. I was mystified.

Just as I was about to shake the whole experience off as some fluke or mental strain due to my bereavement, my little sister who heard the whole conversation, look over at me and shouted out, "I saw her! I saw the Lady!"

"You saw her? You saw the lady I was talking to?"

"Yes," she replied.

Whew, I was relieved! For a minute, I almost thought I was going mad!

"Where did she go?" I inquired.

My sister shrugged her shoulders, and said "uh-uh-dunno!"

I left it at that, because now I would look for

the mysterious lady at the family place where everyone was gathering after the funeral. Surely, she
would be there. Although I did not know how, she
must have gotten in someone's car before I could see
her. After arriving at the family's place there was a
spread of food laid out on the table so thick it looked
like Thanksgiving. So much food, family and friends
were there but no sight of our mystery lady.

Connecting with Hattie

One thing that was left in my mind, I got to
connect with Hattie. Perhaps she could make sense of
all this; with regard to my experience of the disap-
pearing mystery lady.

Certainly the experience did open my mind to
seek what is possible about life and those things
which are not always explainable by logical means.

I stayed up late talking to Hattie. She seemed
to have a lot of answers to the questions I was seeking. She seemed to know a lot about God, the Holy
Spirit and spiritual stuff. I found her quite interesting. We met in the eighth grade. She always seemed
way mature beyond her years. I felt Hattie was the
one of my peer group that I could share my unusual
experience with and she would know what it was all
about.

She was always asking me to visit church with
her, but church always felt unnatural to me. It was
like a show, a place you go to get entertained. I think
I was watching for years the contrast between Catholic school and the Baptist church. Each one stated
that their way is the only one true way.

To be honest neither felt like the path for me. So when Hattie started asking me to go visit her church, I was reluctant to say the least. Yet, there was something about her that made me curious.

"Why don't you come to church with me and you will see?" Hattie said.

"Because I feel a lot of people in the Church are confused when it comes to God. There are so many religions nobody seems to know what the real truth is, including me. I don't even know if there is such a thing as God?" I could see Hattie was now concerned about my response.

Yet she seemed determined to shine some light on my confusion. "Yes, God is very much real. You got to get to get to know Him."

"Well, how do I do that?" I did not understand how that was possible. She explained about God as if God was a male waiting to come down to meet me personally, and He was at this Church she goes to.

I thought about it. I hated going to any church, in my past experiences it felt like a lot of begging was going on for money. I saw that shiny offering plate get passed around, up and down the aisle several times. Then it seemed like the talks were long, drawn out, and to say the least, boring. Church was hardly a place that seemed to know about God. Every week, I had heard conflicting information from both Churches about God. I was thinking if this is true, what I am hearing, why are they saying different things? Perhaps, they are talking about two different Gods.

One thing I did not need was more confusion in my head about God or religion. Hattie was now offering me yet a different church from the other two. This sounded even more confusing. I went from believing in no god at all to an angry vengeful god, to a god who will forgive you if you confess to another man in a small pine box. It never made sense. It never felt right. At my young age I knew the things being said about God were not true. I had no one around me who truly felt the same way. Something about Hattie's Church seemed different. It was worth more investigation.

I was in strict opposition to believing everything about God. I wanted and needed proof. It is not about believing, it is about knowing. I noticed in observing nature it showed me more truth about God than believing what someone said.

The Roast Beef Principle

It is like the story of the granddaughter who continued the tradition of cutting the ends of roast beef and throwing it in the trash. She only followed the process her mother taught her how to cook roast beef. One day the granddaughter asked her Grandma, "Why is the roast beef cooked that way, is it to make it easier to cook?"

The Grandmother laughed, "No my child. It is because years ago I only had one small pan, and had to cut off both ends off the roast beef to make it fit."

My question is, am I following tradition based on past assumptions of God based on the Roast Beef Principle? I had to be sure. I continued to question everything.

My response to Hattie was, "I don't know, I have been to Church and I did not find God there. I did not like it. Everybody was dressing like a fashion show from one church. I saw a woman one time wearing a stuff fox around her neck. It looked so real I thought I could see the eyes still blinking on it!"

Hattie broke out in a laugh.

"You don't have to worry about that at my church- people don't care what you wear." She said convincingly.

"Com-on, of course they do, you mean I can come there naked, huh?"

Hattie laughed some more, "No, silly."

"You know what I mean, clothes are superficial. We are not like that. We are more concerned about the message of God than being concerned about what people wear." Also, my Pastor is a woman."

"A woman, I never heard of a woman Pastor before?" My mouth dropped in amazement. This church sounded unusual to say the least.

It unnerved me a little that my friend was so fanatical about going to Church.

She was persuasive. I admit, I was curious, I never saw a woman Pastor in action before. It seemed like God only had a liking to men bringing forth the messages, based on my past experiences in church. I had to see this woman Pastor.

A Mystery Angel?

I asked Hattie about the mystery lady, and she said the mystery lady had to be an Angel from heaven. Hattie said, "Mystery Angels come into people's lives all the time to deliver messages and then disappear. The Bible mentions in the text and says: "be careful how you entertain strangers, some of us have spoken to Angels unaware."

I said, "Well she certainly gave me a very important message!" It changed my life forever.

Before long, I was visiting church with Hattie. The Pastor was riveting and dynamic. In church they were talking about getting saved, but I was not convinced. I never heard my Grandma talking about getting saved. Although, I heard her praying out loud every night, I believed she was talking with the Angels and the Ancestors. My Grandma was talking out loud and speaking very earnestly in her requests. I felt through power of her prayers she was communicating with someone.

In going to Church with Hattie, I began to take serious interests in learning about the spiritual realm and God. I did this because, I said I would. I promised the mystery lady. I know by meeting her there is another place where our departed ones go when they leave this earth. I had to learn all about this place where my mystery lady and Grandma went.

Finally... a Confirmation from my Sister

It was years later when my sister would confide in me, not wanting to admit what she had really seen that day. I think what she saw frightened her. Finally, after a little coaxing from me, she reviled what she remembered of her experience on that strange, mysterious day.

My little sister said she actually saw the mysterious lady evaporate in thin air! The lady actually ascended in the air as she disappeared. My sister was my only witness for no one else saw the lady. I had asked everyone who showed up at the family gathering after the funeral if they saw me talking to the lady by the tree, at the cemetery. Everyone had the same answer-"No."

I never saw her name in my Grandmother's phone book and I never saw her again. Perhaps one day I will see her again, on that great day when it is my turn leave this body behind. I pray I will see her and my Grandma again.

Reflecting and Learning
from the Experience

I thought long and hard over what the mystery lady had shared with me that day! It was a pivotal point in my life. I was very depressed at my Grandma's passing. I felt I had nothing to live for at that time. After she spoke with me, I had hope again in this life and now the next life. I had something to live for. This is a real story. The events did occur just as I stated them. Only my sister and I were witnesses to this mysterious visitor who appeared as easy as she disappeared. She taught me there was proof of another world, and that it sometimes melds in with our physical world.

I am eternally grateful for her special message. She was proof that there is another place and realm that is unseen from our natural world and eyes. I knew instinctively that this unseen realm does interact with us all the while. It does affect our lives and also our level of wellness. Once I understood there is more to this world than what I can see, it gave me comfort. To access the spiritual or unseen realm is what we do all the time through our thoughts. It is where our creative power and the world of *what is possible* reside.

What is possible? Everything!

Yes, everything is truly possible. Our souls live beyond the body. To be wise is to be spiritual. To be spiritual is to understand the true purpose of our soul in this realm. The important message is that life changes as you believe, and knowing there is a higher power sustains us and gives us authority to embrace life. This helped me to lose my fear of death, knowing this other world exists and family members go there.

Yes, the mystery lady taught me there was proof that there is another world. She helped me to see another perspective, and I'm eternally grateful.

Note to Self: *To understand the mystery of creation is to understand the Eternal.*

Chapter 9:

Female, Male and *More:* The All in All

We live in two worlds simultaneously. Actually we live in more, but that is another topic for another book.

To understand nature and our natural world is understand the creative force that designed it. Some people call the creative force *God, Jesus, Allah, Jehovah, Buddha, Christna, The Christ, Confucius, Ra, Ausar, Obatala,* or *The Universe.*

As I started out in the different churches- I learned everyone has a story to define the Divine Creator. Could it be everyone from different cultures and persuasion were talking about the same thing? They were only telling the story from their understanding?

As I began studying the different religions- or their meanings (the ways of life). I found a common thread that runs through all of them. There is a natural order to the construct of the universe.

All things were created to express the reflection

of the one who created them. We, too, are here to create life, and live abundantly in happiness, love, peace and joy. All of the religions talk about and an afterlife.

The Divine Creation

Our worlds are broken down into the internal and external. The external world is everything you experience with your physical senses. It is what you see, touch, feel, smell and taste with those senses. The internal world is made up of your thoughts, beliefs, your inner voice, imaginations, interpretations, rationalizations, judgments and dreams.

There are also two main forces used in creation and co-creation. These forces are represented as the Male and Female energies. Male and female were made in the image of the one who created them. Therefore the Creator must be and have attributes of both male and female. The Father and Mother expressions exist in all and everything in nature.

How can we label the Great, Omnipotent Creator? Something so vast remains nameless. It is the Great I Am that I Am. (The Grand All in All). It lives in everyone. It is everywhere and in everything.

When I discovered the designer in the design, I began by studying nature. By my observation of nature and being in nature I began to notice distinct patterns. Nature became one of my greatest teachers. For nature is the handiwork and creation of the Divine Designer in all things.

The male creation is also known as the 'seen' realm and the female creation is also known as the 'unseen' realm. In Asian philosophy, they teach about *yin* and *yang* energy, which is female-yin and male yang. These energies are inherent in everything. Each energy has the presence of its opposite in it.

In the yin and the yang symbol you will notice that in the circle there is a black dot that represents yin in the white space (yang), and in the black space (yin) there is a white dot (yang). It is a symbol representing the balance of life. It shows in the feminine the masculine is present. In the masculine the feminine is there as well.

As in human expressions of male and female, there are both male hormones and female hormones in everyone. The dominant expression of male or female is due to the highest amount of gender hormone present in the body at the time. In some human beings there are equal expressions of each hormone present.

These human beings are known as hermaphrodites, having both genders expressed physically and present. Also, if a male wishes to grow breasts he can do so by receiving female hormone injections. If female wishes to have more male traits, like facial hair and a deeper voice, she can do so by receiving male hormone injections.

Females have a distinct energy and males have a distinct energy. Each needs to be cultivated to bring true harmony to the body.

There are habits that are considered regenerating to female energy and there are energies that are cultivating and regenerating to male energy.

Note to Self: Understand the characteristics of energy. This unlocks the keys to creation.

According to the biblical account, the Creator made male and female and called them Adam and Eve.

This is an ancient Chinese symbol for energy. The black part of the circle represents female energy. The white part of the circle represents male energy. There is female in male and male in the female. It is an all-encompassing circle that never ends.

The Female YIN Energy

The feminine exemplifies the magnetic quality, a force for drawing and attracting. It is the energy of The Great Unseen, everything that is unseen. Its qualities are invisible force, internal awareness, darkness, soft, subtle, flexible, pliable, water, winter, passive, smooth, intuitive, nurturing, contracting, creative, right brained, flowing, obscure, night, resting, sleeping, etc.

The days with the highest yin energies are: Monday, Wednesday, Friday and Saturday. It is interesting that the Sabbath day is related our Saturday. It is considered the last day of the week. It is a yin day. Yin days are excellent for resting, praying and going within. It is interesting that The Sabbath day is considered a day of rest. Saturday is energetically aligned to reset the mind, body and soul through rest.

Society has taught us not to give creditability to what is unseen. Basically, what is unseen represents the female characteristics and the female energies. It is an old notion that what is not picked up by the five senses does not exist in reality. But, in fact, this is not true. In recognizing subtle energies one has to consider that which is unseen. Everything that is seen came from the unseen.

Human beings are composed of both male and female energies. To live a balanced life one must be able to connect with both. It is important to recognize the female energy as part of life, and work with it. The female energy is needed in creation as nature teaches us. It nurtures and supports growth and harmony.

The Male YANG Energy

This energy exemplifies the quality of electrical, stimulating and generating. It is of The Great Seen, everything that is visible to the eyes. Its characteristics are visible force, external awareness, lightness, hard, forthright, blunt, fire, summer, bold, ragged, sharp, expansive, boxed in, concentrated, analytical, left brained, day, awake, etc. The days of the week with the highest yang energy are Sunday, Tuesday and Thursday.

The yin and yang energies and qualities of each function of male and female are designed from creation. Both are needed. When studying human male and female, the same thing applies. Society encourages us to be yang for production and for work. In western society, it has been a male dominated, focused culture stemming from a male orientation. But both male and female energies are needed within us for balance. When we recognize our vibrations, notice the male and female energies.

Both Energies Together
Bring Completeness

Western society tends to be patriarchal male energy dominated. We see this present in religion, as God is always referred to as He or Him. There is the father and son, but no mother and daughter. In nature, there is always male and female energy present for creation to flow. We have been taught to believe that the real power lies in being male. We need to work with and recognize the importance of both energies.

Diseases are formed when one is out of harmony with his or her natural energy. In fact, it is empowering for the female to be female energy dominated, for that is where her real power is; and the male is to be dominant in male energy, for that is where his real power is. Both must know how and when to allow the opposite energy to flow.

In regards to the male hormone, what makes a man physically male is an abundance of testosterone. That is accountable for semen, male reproductive organs, deep voice, and facial hair. The female hormones progesterone and estrogen makes the female a bio-female. These hormones or bio-chemicals cause breast development, lactation and menstruation. As stated before, in each male and female there are hormones of the other present: testosterone hormones in small amounts in the female and estrogen in small amounts in the male. Male energy is needed in the process of creation.

The male energy brings forth the raw, physical energy necessary for concrete results. Without it creation cannot express itself in the sensory world. Female energy is also needed in the nurturing of creation. The female energy is needed in cultivating the spiritual and emotional resources necessary for expression in the physical world.

A Gender Basis for
All Creation

We as human beings have both male and female and *more*. What makes a female or a male depends on the amount of male and female hormones present and how much male or female energy is expressed.

In all things, there is a blending of male and female vibrational creative quality.

This amazing power came from the Divine Creator who is both male and female and *more!*

There are instances in this book where I refer to God as Source Energy, Christ energy, and Mother-Father Creator. I will explain why.

In my journeys and working with Source energy. I have discovered *as above so below*, meaning that the Creator in Earth's creation used male and female energy to have a successful creation. A human has never been created through two males or two females. It has always been one male and one female that came together sexually and then another human is created. This principle is very important to understand. It is the basis of all creation.

To create anything, one must have male and female energy and actions present. This may not be an easy concept to grasp at first, but once understood you can create anything you believe is possible.

One must believe it- think it and visualize it (female principle because those things are all unseen), then you must put physical action behind what you believe, thought and visualize (male principle because actions are seen). Put all that together and, 'WHALLA,' expressed creation occurs. You see, if you desire, you can, even to be healed you can. If you desire to have wealth you can!

The Perfect Creation

In every perfect creation male and female energy is used. By studying nature's true handiwork and reflection one observes that the Divine is present in everything. There is not one human or animal on this planet that did not come without a male and a female process. I know the aspects of the Creator are male and female and more. The creator is neither male nor female, as source energy-for the Divine Creator encompasses both. I do not know of anything that exists on this planet that did not get here by design. Someone, some being, thought about it then created it. A true creation that is stable needs both male and female energy to exist.

A Lesson in Developing Balance

Through my body's challenges, I began to discover the Creator's purpose for the body. That was to be in balance. Healing occurred when both male and female energies were in perfect balance and in harmony with nature.

Let me explain what I am saying: since we are energetic beings we respond to these male / female energies all the time. If we do not keep them in balance sickness ensues. This balance is like living in the reality that night balances the day, and sleeping balances being awake.

Also meditation balances out the mind of an analytical thinker. Exercise balances out stagnant energy. Peace balances out war.

With every male energy activity, a female energy activity is there for balancing and vice versa. All things move in form and function through the female and male creative process.

Everything on the earth is birthed through this

male and female creative process. Each has its purpose and one is dependent on the other for balanced, effective results.

Nature has made it that way.

A balanced and healthy lifestyle comes from aligning with this reality and embracing one's true energies and purpose.

Note to Self: As I monitor my thoughts to be more positive, I create a more positive and fulfilling life. SaEnya

Chapter 10:

Energy and Vibration

The breath, as discussed earlier, draws the Life-Force into our bodies, and provides unseen nutrition for the body, mind and Great Spirit within each of us. Our very thoughts, then, are dependent upon the energy received from the breath.

Breath, Thought and Vibration

There are several different levels of vibrational thought. Thinking within these various levels produces certain types of reactions and can lead your life towards stress and sickness, or wellbeing and health. Every thought vibrates to a pitch and a sound and is invoked by a color.

There are seven primary levels of being that generate classification of thoughts: These levels of being – called *chakras* – are vibratory levels that correspond to where people energetically reside. I will briefly comment on those levels below, beginning with the base chakra or survival energy:

Vibrational Thought Levels

●<u>Level I: Animalistic/Instinctual</u>: At this level, pictured as the lowest ball in the above illustration, the quality of thoughts is *basic survival*. Food, shelter, water and safety, the basic frequencies of thoughts at this level, are all vibrating to survive by any means necessary. The individual at this level is very self-serving. Children who were abused by their parents or abandoned by their parents can stay stuck at this level for a long time. The main inference of thought is *kill or be killed*. The main beliefs are concepts like "It's a dog eat dog world. I come first before anybody. No one is to be trusted. Love does not exist."

The energetic core of this frequency is "I must

do anything I can to survive." No consideration is given to the impact on others when choices are made for the individual's survival interests. Power from this level is generated and motivated by self-directed interests.

Energetic Correlation: This vibratory Level I corresponds to Chakra #1, which is the base chakra with its color red. It resonates with the sound '*Doe*' and heavy base level sounds. This energy is seen in mentally and emotionally challenged persons, newborn babies, homeless people, and Alzheimer diagnosed persons. At this level the person has difficulty forming meaningful relationships. In later stages of life the person may lack connection to purpose and real happiness. There are often blood challenges, air exchange challenges and structural (Bone) challenges.

●Level II: Tribal/Animated: At this level thoughts are based on the *tribe*. This could be a smaller community, a particular race that one belongs to, a church or religious affiliation, a cult or organization, family, team, corporate tribe or gang. Everything is about that group or affiliation. Whatever the tribe collectively wants or believes in is accepted as what is right.

Belonging to the tribe is what the thoughts are primarily about. Pleasing the tribe and belonging is what is most important. The main inference of thought is "I will die for the tribe, I will protect the tribe, I will kill for the tribe. I am only loyal to the tribe. Only my religious way is right." Tribal mentality is wishing harm or thinking harm will come to all other groups that are outside the clan or affiliation.

Most gang and cult members' thoughts vibrate at this level. At this level agreements and bonds formed may be harmful to others and ultimately the persons themselves. Tribal persons can be superstitious, believing in good and bad magical spirits or the casting of magic spells to influence events and curses to control others outside the group. Some are prone to cult rituals that harm themselves, animals, or other persons.

Energetic Correlation: This vibratory Level II-corresponds to Chakra #2, the sacral chakra. This chakra vibrates to connectivity. There is a strong desire for creativity, and to connect together with like-minded persons. The color here is orange, and the vibrational sound is 'Ray'. This energy is observed in love sick persons, separation anxiety persons, and spleen challenged persons. Reproductive organs play a key role in feeling and responding to this energy.

●Level III: Power Deity/Narcissistic: The frequency of thoughts at this level shows the first emergence of the will. The person at this level has moved beyond the tribe and cult survival mentality, and the sacral needs, and is now beginning to exercise free will thinking outside of the group or society norms. The thoughts here can be impulsive, egocentric, ethnocentric, powerful, influential over others, and even heroic.

These are the 'Go Getters' in the world. They tend to go for what they want in life. Persons of this vibrational frequency can appear power hungry, with high ego power. The stream of thoughts are "No one is better than me. I am a God or Goddess in my own

116

right. I control my world and everything and everyone in it. How can I get ahead to the next level?"

Persons vibrating at this level are high achievers. They felt it necessary to prove something to the world to get validation of 'who and what' they are. They can be considered control freaks. Very immovable on what they think is right. They do not care what other people think or feel.

These persons might have limited viewpoints, unable to see the other person's point of view. They can exhibit a low level of reasoning and understanding of others. Relationships formed are based on control not love. The relationship is based on how can this person best serve me and my desires and wants in life? If the relationship does not honor, serve or reflect that person's goals, it may well be severed without a second thought.

<u>Energetic Correlation</u>: This vibratory level III-corresponds to Chakra #3, the solar plexus chakra. Its color is yellow; its sound is 'Me'. This energy is evident in high powered entertainers, ambitious politicians, military leaders, high ranking religious leaders, highly paid consultants, exceptional athletes, corporate leaders, recognized business owners, international award winning people, and independent and rebellious teenagers. This energy can lead to intestinal and digestive challenges if one is careless with his or her health.

●<u>Level IV: Philanthropist/Zealous Order:</u> At this level one begins to seek truth and the meaning of life, and is committed to begin living truth as it becomes more clearly defined. The world of agreement starts here.

Integrity and building relationships based on truth and honesty takes on importance. The person begins to think about how outcomes and actions affect others rather than just the self. Thoughts on this frequency are "How can I make a contribution to the world that will make a positive difference? How can I make the Earth a better place?"

The person moves from being self-centered to beginning to being altruistic. There is an attraction to philanthropy, higher spiritual thoughts, and ways of being. There is a wanting to do what right and balanced. This person exhibits a strong sense of right, wrong, and duty. He or she begins to put responsible actions over emotions, now looking to contribute to life in meaningful ways.

<u>Energetic Correlation</u>: This vibratory level IV corresponds Chakra #4, the heart chakra. The representative colors are green and pink. The sound is 'Fa'. Here we find persons who truly feel the needs and hopes of others in their hearts. They contribute to the homeless, relate to humanitarian causes, are animal and earth rights activists; they may work as nurses, firefighters, school teachers, community volunteers, philanthropists and other service focused professions.

A person at this level will usually exhibit high moral standards, and a heart-felt willingness to promote civic harmony with responsibility.

●<u>Level V: Structure/Creation:</u> At this level the person is very knowledgeable and understands universal law and how he creates his own reality. This vibrational level encourages open communication and creativity skills to promote ones vision and bring about change that benefits a greater community, or a growing number of people. Achievements at this level can cause positive transformation in the world. The person accepts responsibility not only for his actions but for the actions of others. The vibration of thoughts at this level, "How did I cause this? How can I change this in a way that will benefit the world?"

Energetic Correlation: This vibrational level V corresponds to Chakra #5, the throat chakra represented by the color blue; its sound is 'SO'. This is our communication and creativity of expression center, meaning persons can be very vocal, activists, abstract thinkers, high level leaders for change. Thyroid challenges can manifest at this energy lever.

●Level VI: Visionary/Intuitive: At this level the individual has a world view. How will my actions impact the seen and unseen worlds? These persons know that real power for creating is in seeding the unseen realm. They work with their visions and dreams to make them manifest on Earth. These visions and dreams usually come from the higher dimensions. These visions have been the seeds for modern day inventions, fashions, design, arts and architecture.

Energetic Correlation: This level VI corresponds to Chakra #6, the third eye chakra. Its color is indigo (blue/violet); its sound is 'LA'. This chakra energy increases ones psychic, intuitive abilities and capacity for seeing multiple viewpoints. This level of vibrational thinking is seen in outstanding leaders.

These include visionaries, highly creative persons, priests, priestesses and those adept in working in the unseen spiritual realm. Those at this energy level can experience health issues with the Pituitary and brain.

●Level VII; God-Self/Open Channel: Individuals at this level are connected to their *higher selves*. They are spiritually in tune with themselves and their Source. They are altruistic persons who are guided by their higher selves, and by channeled higher spiritual guides and forces. They are led by the voice from within and have a holistic viewpoint of the world.

They tend to see the world from a higher perspective. They are here on the earth to channel the higher frequencies of Source Energy. They know that they are here to raise the vibration of the earth's social structure. When earth's vibrations are raised to this 7th frequency or level, this high vibrational network of beings will have manifested heaven on Earth.

All tears will be wiped away. There will be no more pain or victimhood, because it cannot and does not reside at this level.

Energetic Correlation: This high vibrational level corresponds to Chakra #7, the crown chakra. Its color is violet/or red-violet, or can be whitish crystal; its sound is *Ti or Si'*, and corresponds to the pineal gland, the master timing gland. Everything moves in divine timing and cycles. This level of vibrational thought is seen in master sages, high spiritual teachers and world leaders with a high level of integrity. They are prime movers in this world, but ignoring their own wellbeing can give rise to mental depression and psychosomatic challenges.

Remember the admonition: *Be transformed by the renewal of your mind (from the* New Testament).

Creating Health and Happiness

It is important to only think on those things that you really want to see happen. As you identify the things you wish to have happen, energize them with your emotions and feelings.

When you are consistent with a particular thought, you are energizing that thought to manifest in your physical reality! This is how we become conscious co-creators with the Eternal, Divine Creator.

Our thoughts become words and our words shape and create our worlds! This is activating the law of attraction in our life. Each person has the ability to change the level of vibrational thoughts flowing through the mind. It is like directing the mind into a flowing channel at a particular level of vibration.

If you want to vibrate at a high vibrational frequency, raise the level of your thoughts to consistently reside at that level. If a lower vibrational thought comes to mind, nullify it by replacing it with a higher vibrational thought of gratitude or acceptance. Focus on the level of thought you wish to maintain. Then park your mind and thoughts there. You will then increasingly draw that level of thought to you. Those thoughts will begin to manifest circumstances that match the level of your thinking.

They say *birds of a feather flock together.* People who have a consistent level of thought frequencies tend to draw others into their space, time and energy. So, changing your thoughts will change your life.

The Energy Guidance System

Your physical body gives you guidance through your awareness. It also guides you by your energy levels. Do you consistently have low energy? Energy responds to those who listen to the voice of their bodies.

If your energy is low or waning, check out *why*. Ask yourself, "Have I been honoring myself in what I wish to create for my life?"

If not, breathe it in. Be with the feelings that are present within you. By *feeling* creation, it allows you greater access to your awareness, consciousness and being. Be kind to yourself and love yourself unconditionally. Start out by saying every morning, "I love my life. I like myself. I like my life. I love myself."

Call those things that be not as though they were. This allows the bio-chemicals to work more freely and seamlessly without hampering the energy flow. Allow by knowing it is OK whatever you may be going through. It is Ok, you are experiencing exactly what you are to experience right now. Everything you are experiencing or creating is perfect, no matter what it may look like or feel like. And know that you are calling those things you desire into being

Note to Self: I become what I constantly think about!

Chapter 11:

Creating with Unseen Energies

The body is an amazing physical, emotional and mental structure. It connects us to seen and unseen forces.

These unseen forces gain access to our body through thoughts. Our thoughts actually create portals that connect us to our purest intention. As these thoughts continue along the same continuous stream, they begin to have an emotional charge to them.

Like Attracts Like

These charges attract more of the same, and all connect to the body either positively or negatively. The body then responds in harmony or disharmony, according to the frequency of the thought. When the thought is based on truth the body responds harmoniously. When the thought is based on non-truth, disharmony ensues.

Appreciation draws more things to appreciate in one's life. And so it is for everything else.

Like attracts like. Suspend all judgment and observe.

When the body responds in disharmony for a period of time dis-ease follows. As it was pointed out earlier, it actually takes on average three minutes of continuous thought for that particular thought to become a part of our physical structure. Depending on the nature of the disharmonious thoughts and feelings, a particular disease is invoked. It causes a particular pattern.

I like to simply call the thoughts *energy*. When energy is felt it becomes vibration.

The type of vibrations that I am speaking of is generated within and is felt without, using energy from the 'etheric world' or 'unseen world' and made manifest in the physical world.

Receiving and Transmitting

Imagine our bodies as transmitters able to receive and send frequencies. These frequencies can create wellness or sickness. That is how thoughts can actually cause wellbeing or physical illness.

My own healing began the day I started thinking and saying, "I am healed." Today I am disease free! Give thanks to the Divine Creator and my Ancestors!

Note to Self: You are what you say and feel you are!

I learned, first hand, that disharmonious emotions affect our organs and create disease. Here are some reminders of the power of thoughts:

"We cannot solve our problems with the same thinking we used when we created them"-Albert Einstein.

"Whatsoever things are true, whatsoever things are honest, whatsoever things are just, whatsoever things are pure, whatsoever things are lovely, and whatsoever things are of good report: if there be any virtue, and if there be any praise, think on these things." KJV PHP 4:8

"Death and Life are in the power of the tongue: and they that love it shall eat the fruit thereof." KJV PR 18:21

Note to Self: thoughts become things, for thoughts can become words and words shape and create our world!

The Unseen Body Language

How do thoughts create disease or create health? Each organ in our bodies resonates with a 'thought- vibration expression.'

Each organ is affected physically by a particular feeling. These feeling have encoded in them a frequency that affect the organ that resonates with that thought frequency. Each organ has a distinct vibrational resonance.

These feelings or vibrational expression causes

particular results listed in the chart below. Low vibration means holding negative thought patterns over an extended period of time. High vibrational expressions or high vibrational thoughts mean holding a positive thought patterns over an extended period of time.

Again, I point out that it takes on average three minutes of holding a particular thought vibration for it to change the vibratory level in one's harmonic frequency. This is one reason why it is so important to think positive thoughts, as thoughts affect the vibration of each organ in a particular way. Eliminate discomforting thoughts. I found it helpful to simply practice being lovely and gracious.

Take inventory of your emotions. They are the gateway to your health and will assist you in your healing. Acknowledge them. They hold the key to understanding your conversations that empower you or dis-empower you.

You are a vibrational being, your vibration is the key to your inner kingdom. Understand your body's code and language. It will give you a clear map into yourself. Know that you are what you eat, think, and speak. Begin now by speaking life, healing and love into your existence.

The most successful people in life had to be slightly delusional. They had to believe more in the dream than in their physical reality. They had to have more courage to believe in the dream than what reality dictated. They followed the dream by applying action to make it real. A dream without action continues to remain a dream. If your dream is to heal, follow your inner leading whole heartily. You will be successful if you continue on your path.

Once the desire is there, your body, mind and soul joins together to actualize what you are asking for.

This is what is meant that *you must remain as a child to enter the kingdom.* Children believe in dreams; they are not hard wired to reality. Adults believe in perceived reality more than their dreams. The dreams lie in the inner kingdom, where your soul reigns. You have the dream because something inside you knows it is possible. It is where the realm of possibility inhabits.

So, keep dreaming my friend; keep on knowing a change is going to come.

What You Focus On You Attract

At the back of your brain you have what is called the RAS system (the *reticular activating system*). Its job is to filter out all the unimportant things from your conscious mind. It allows you to focus on and see only the things you deem important.

Right now your skin is measuring how hot or cold your environment is. It is also measuring how the clothes are feeling on your body. Your eyes are measuring the light or absence of light in the room as you read this book. Your stomach is digesting food or sensing the absence of food.

Your liver is making chemicals to store or break down food. Your hair and nails are growing. You ears are sensing sounds. Your feet are feeling how tight your shoes are on your feet, if you have on shoes. Your organs are receiving and responding to various emotions and vibrational energies.

127

The Chart Below Shows the Effects of Vibration on Your Organs

Organ	Low vibrational Feelings:	High vibrational Feelings:
Bladder	Stagnation	Accomplishment/ Flow
Gallbladder	Bitterness	Forgiveness
Heart	Mistrust/doubt	Faith/trust
Kidney	Fear	Courage
Liver	Anger	Peace
Lung	Grief/Sorrow	Rapture/Ecstasy
Pancreas	Unhappiness	Joy
Intestine (Small)	Rejection	Integration
Intestine (Large)	Attachment	Detachment
Spleen	Unfulfilled desire	Fulfillment
Stomach	Aversion	Acceptance
Endocrine Glands	Imbalance	Harmony
Reproductive	Unproductive	Creativity

There are thousands of things right now occurring in and around you that are vying for your attention. If you were to consciously focus on everything you would go through sensory overload and breakdown.

So thank goodness you have the RAS doing its job – filtering out the more mundane or less critical things from your consciousness so you can focus on the things that you consciously wish to draw into your awareness.

This is one of the important reasons for writing down your goals, then reading them and focusing on them. Not only are you activating the law of attraction, but you are physically programing your RAS databank to alert you when the goals are present or the opportunity to access your goals are within your reach.

Your *Right-Now* Feelings

Become aware of whatever emotions you are feeling *right now*. If they are low vibrational, use the following chart to determine what organ these emotions are effecting. Then, send loving energy to that organ.

For example, if you have been experiencing unhappiness, you will see that chronic unhappiness effects the pancreas. After a while this can trigger the disease of diabetes. This has been proven through studies in Chinese medicine. Likewise, every thought will either decrease the life force or will increase the life force of a particular organ.

The 'unseen' realm affects the 'seen' realm;

and the root cause of all disease starts in the *unseen* realm with the thoughts and feelings.

These unseen thoughts and feelings will then manifest into what is the *seen* realm, providing evidence once again, that the inner is reflected in the outer.

Note to Self: I am manager and architect of my life; I will manage and design it to be whole, sound and well.

Chapter 12:

Finding True Purpose

Every thought is a prayer that is broadcast out into the universe. The universe, which means literally ONE-SONG, is listening to our prayers. Consider that we are channels, *broadcasting and receiving,* for the divine.

'Every thought is a Prayer. Thoughts are prayers in consciousness.'– Lisa I.

Prayers are answered through our belief. You ask anything believing it and you shall receive it. This works with the law of attraction. The law of attraction is causing events and circumstances to occur in our life by virtue of energy calling forth what we believe we deserve and desire to have happen.

When belief is activated by something we are thinking about, something spoken or something you are creating, the law of attraction is activated in our

lives. Ask for what you desire and you will have it.
So, the question arises, "If all this is true, why is it that what I desire and have asked for has not come to past?"

Conflicting Thoughts

The answer lies in this truth: When you broadcast out what you desire, then a vibrational match is also needed to receive what it is that you have requested.

If you are not a vibrational match for what you have asked for, it will be delayed in coming to you until you are a vibrational match for what you have requested. This works for everything that you have requested, asked, spoken, imagined, or written. It works with consistency on all mediums of communicating being our thoughts, written words, imaginations, and requests.

Like A Prayer

We gather energy or loose energy through our habits and thoughts. Prayer assists us in focusing our requests to be manifested. We are here to produce an effect in harmony with our true purpose for being here. Each one of us has a unique purpose to produce in life the thing that has brought us here in the first place. It is my responsibility to seek out and find my true purpose, my destiny. Once I have found my true purpose I am accountable in manifesting it.

This brings true happiness and wellness in life.

What is your true purpose? It is built into each one of us to lead us to satisfaction and true joy.

Starting True Work or
Life's Purpose

You may ask yourself, why am I here? Everything has a unique purpose that only you are here to do.

How do you discover your true, unique purpose? It is like looking in the mirror one must seek and look by spending time with yourself. By meditating and asking, praying, and focusing, your true purpose will show itself.

Most disease and unhappiness is generated by not understanding or knowing one's true purpose, or having the courage to follow one's true purpose.

In my own case, I came to realize my true purpose was sharing the knowledge of health and wealth with others. This gives me great joy. But, I got caught up in fear because I could not see how I could physically support myself by expressing or sharing my true purpose with those willing to hear.

The thought came to me that I also needed a job for income. But a job is just that – a *job*. It pays the bills, yet I was so unhappy, day in and out going to this one particular job. I felt trapped. Then it got worse! I got sick- I was diagnosed with an ulcer. I was vomiting, nauseous. I could not eat.

The pattern continued I lost weight. Eventually, my doctor admitted me in the hospital. I asked the Divine Creator what I can do to change the current picture. The answer came clear as a bell, *step out in faith*. Believe in yourself. Move forward one step at a time. I followed the direction and soon I was making a living doing what I love. To live life fully demands courage.

To get an idea of your life's purpose, get a pencil and paper and follow these simple steps. Start by making a list of the following:

1. Things that make you very happy;
2. Things you love to do;
3. Things you can do and don't notice the time;
4. Things you can do or do not mind doing all day and do not need compensation for it. Like you can do it and not need to get paid for it, although getting paid for it would be a very nice gesture.

The answers will be different for everyone. There is no right or wrong with this little exercise. And, it is best to suspend judgment of the things you like to do. You are what you are.

After writing those things down, begin to note the things in common. Notice the things that you have a connection with. As you focus on each item, notice as you breathe in and out, the things you wrote down that give you the biggest smile; the things that make you feel very good. Then circle those things.

This may take some time, so be patient with yourself. Find the common thread in the circled words that generate the most joy within you. The common thread is your theme; it indicates what you would like to contribute by being here.

The next step is to express that in your life's work, then you have found your purpose and are putting it into action! Expressions of purposes are not static. They fluctuate in time. But the common theme still applies if it is your true purpose.

For me, I realized that my true purpose was in

wealth, health and healing. No matter what I chose to do, the activities in life where I found the most joy always circled back around to that expression.

There are degrees of purpose in life. We have seen how some have achieved great satisfaction by being truly focused on great achievement that not only made a difference in their life, but made a difference in the lives of others. These brave persons impacted themselves and others in a profound and positive way.

Remember, too, that the whole purpose of expressing your purpose is to be happy! If you are not happy expressing your purpose, then it is not really your purpose. We were created to be happy, joyous, peaceful and free.

I have observed that sickness is also manifested by one not knowing their true purpose in life, or once they know their purpose they are not actively pursuing it. They are acting on other's purposes or forgoing their purpose because they are afraid to manifest it. This innate fear slowly kills the body, mind, and emotions over time.

Happiness From Within

The true purpose of life is to be happy. True happiness comes from within. External things do make us happy, but that happiness is only temporary.

What continuously allows us to be happy is the happiness that we learn to generate from within.

Loving and being very happy with 'who' and 'what' we are is the place of our natural happiness. Allowing it to flow no matter what the external circumstances are, or what we own or don't own, who we

135

are with and who we are not with, provides the results we truly seek. It is from within, for we are the ones we have been waiting for!

The Energetic Environment

The energetic environment around you can drain your energy like a car battery when you leave your lights on. Being around those who do not encourage you, negative thoughts, people, or situations, and lack of light can drain your energy.

Even the cleanliness and organization of your physical space can affect your energies, accomplishments, attitudes, even how your prayers are answered.

There are studies and a lot of information available on the impact of EMF-(electro-magnetic frequencies), how they impact our energetic body. Being around high electrical wiring, electric poles, airline flights, and computer screens can cause certain cancers, mental and physical illness. I found watching the news on TV or the internet about death, damnations, and discouraging world events were very draining for my energy. I found watching TV for long lengths of time on subjects that were not of my life's purpose was draining as well. I needed to maintain the strongest broadcasting frequency for my prayers to be fully effective. I needed to turn off and at times unplug the TV. I notice I feel better in an energy-clean environment.

I encourage you to go into your personal space, whether it is your home, office or school, and notice how you feel when you are there.

Do you feel energized or drained? If energized that is great, for you are in a supportive environment. Or do you feel drained? If so, find out the source. There are energetic tools one can use to identify EMF issues and methods for protection. For this energy can be very harmful to the body rhythms we were talking about in the earlier chapters. There are computer safety screens to place over the computer. There are protective shields and quartz crystals one can use to protect the energy frequencies of the body. Sometimes it is the things we cannot see with the eyes that can hurt us and affect us the most.

Observing Energy

Sometimes we talk to someone and find that suddenly the wind is out of our sails, as they say. We feel drained. The person just energetically drained us.

Or perhaps you ate your favorite food but minutes later you can barely keep your eyes open. The food has energetically drained you. Or you walk into a room of flickering florescent lights and you feel energetically down and don't know why. The experience has drained you energetically. In the winter months when the sun goes down early you might feel depressed and easily agitated. These and other energy thieves can be very draining. It is wise to observe the *what's* and *why's* of how you feel, and take action to keep your energy at a high vibrational level.

Be true to your energetic nature, as it is vitally important to honor yourself in these circumstances. Manage your energy as you manage your life, and will be able to create a fabulous life. If you feel an energy drain, take corrective action; leave the place physically, or rest, or change the food you eat. Are you feeling drained from a person, the space itself, thoughts you been thinking, then place yourself in a different environment. Ask why is this happening, and then listen, for your inner voice will tell you.

I noticed that being around certain people was draining for me, so I began to avoid them and felt better. To myself I had to be true.

Cure for "SAD"

I was raised in a cold, snow ridden city. I noticed by the end of every January through February I was more sad than usual. For no particular reason around January and February I would get unusually down. I would lose interest in school work and I was not feeling naturally like myself.

Then I found that being in the sun made me feel better and more energized. This is called *seasonal affective disorder* or (SAD). Many people suffer from this, but there are a number of things to reverse the discomfort. One is getting more sunshine or full spectrum lighting in the home. Also, taking different supplements and doing light exercises seems to help.

One day, I took it a step further.

I noticed when I connected in prayer to Source Energy within I was happy no matter what month it was. I confirmed that true power comes from relying on the Source Energy within.

We all have access to it. It is always present. It is there to always empower us. Source Energy keeps us strong in our mind, body, and soul. The source of our happiness is feeling it from within – from the inside. It is always there for us!

Note to Self: Observation is the First step to self-mastery and healing. Take inventory of yourself. SaEnya
("Man know thyself"- Plato)

Hitch Your Thoughts to the Stars

Imagine, every thought is a vibration, and those vibrations are manifesting your life. When in a space of thinking "no possibility" or thinking in negative terms, your life will be led by that. When thinking in "possibility terms" and being in a positive focus, your life will be led by that.

So the key is to hitch all your thoughts to a star and let them soar to the positive realm. Imagine wonderful things and take on every consideration, challenge or concern from a positive reference, and this creates possibilities for the miraculous to occur in your life. Try this on and let it be a way of life, and changes in your life will reflect that.

How to Befriend Ourselves

Some people find that keeping a journal is helpful. Perhaps you would like to get a journal and write down how you feel about yourself.

Ask yourself what criticism do I need to let go of? Learn to develop a deep trust and relationship with yourself. How do you begin to clear negative thoughts about yourself?

When we take a personal inventory, we learn how to react towards ourselves during any negative incident.

When the challenges come, we are able to meet them through being loving, forgiving, and developing a kind relationship towards ourselves. I found being playful lightened up my many challenges. They didn't feel so heavy anymore. Children sometimes are our best teachers because they know how to add play into their lives. One minute they can be having challenges and the next they forgot all about the challenges and are back at play again. Knowing how to recapture the positive is a vital key to life's mastery and success.

I notice *'Being'* is an art. Most of us are about doing rather than being. Being is being conscious of ourselves, our thoughts, and our surroundings. Noticing our feelings, thoughts, and moods will allow us to be aware of our etheric vibrations. Etheric vibrations are controlled and manipulated by our dominant thoughts.

Think positive and positive vibrations are drawn to you. Think negative and negative vibrations are drawn to you. These vibrations are subtle energy forms that can lead to wellness when positive or lead to illness when negative.

I remember the day when my thoughts and emotions set my cancer development in motion. It was in the fall, I was very angry with my Dad. I felt that he had betrayed my trust. I was so angry with him that in my anger I said, "I do not want to pass on any more of his genetics to anyone." I felt that he was a bad man who hurt me and my daughter.

One year and a half later I had developed stage

four tumor, ovarian cancer, and had my genetics removed. What is the chance of that? I have since forgiven him and myself for the experience. I personally believe we create profound experiences for the opportunity to practice forgiveness with our loved ones. We co-create with our intentions, desires, thoughts, and vibrations the outcome of our lives.

I had to take ownership of all my life's creative outcomes, for I came to realize that I am the one directing my life. It is like driving a car and going into a ditch. Perhaps ending up in a ditch was not my highest intended outcome, but I am then challenged to get out of the ditch and be more conscious of my driving and intention of where I want to go. The goal is staying on the clear, open road. Our intentions lead us to the ditch or the clear, open road. It is all a choice. We have power to stay ill or to be well.

Using Emotions to Connect
with the Soul

Have you ever been very emotionally upset?

I discovered when one is in the space of emotional upheaval, the soul is rattled. It is tilled like the farmer tills the soil. Anytime a strong emotional charge is used, one begins to make a deep connection to the soul.

I can recall many times observing this experience. In church, while experiencing a deep ecstasy and going into a euphoric state, I felt for the first time my soul was communicating with the Divine. Also, another time while performing *Dan Hak* yoga exercise, I felt my soul making contact with me.

141

It was during such times that I experienced another aspect to who I thought I was.

The church I attended with Hattie was a Pentecostal Church. The Pentecostal Church is filled with emotionally charged energy. I would see the women pastor start shouting in praise to God. The music was alive and loud, including singing that felt like it belted out to the universe. The drums, organ and tambourines were charged with thunderous melodies.

These energies caused the congregation to go into feverish praises and emotional whirlwinds of crying, tied into fits of joy. It was frightening to watch, because I did not understand what was making these women and men start jumping and shouting "Thank you Jesus," as they would contort and run about.

Then I had my own mystical experience. I was sitting in church minding my business when I felt my lower jaw quivering. I found that to be strange. I whispered to Hattie, "There is something going on with my jaw, it's quivering."

She said it was the Holy Ghost wanting to commune with me. She called over the pastor. The pastor said, "Stand up and start shouting, Thank you, Jesus."

I followed her command. It was my intention to finally connect with God. In my shouting, I actually saw a light come down over me. It seemed like only I and the light was there. I felt something so powerful rise up out of me it shook my very foundation. I began to speak with another language. I call it the language of the soul. I began to say thank you to what I called at the time Jesus, and say thank you God for letting me know God is real. I understood what I was saying but it was coming out in another language. I felt in ecstasy like I never felt before. I felt like I was bathed in a million rays of dazzling sunlight. I felt like I was dipped in the eternal spring of life, as these words began to babble and bubble up out of what was previously a dry soul. I felt full after that. I became aware of a warm, loving presence that I was not conscious of before. This presence was always there. It was inside me waiting for me to acknowledge it. Now I felt like the light was on.

After the unusual experience had culminated, the pastor said to me, "You are now filled with the Holy Ghost." She said I was to now conduct myself in a pious and holy way, and not to grieve the Holy Ghost.

One thing this experience did was heighten my listening to what rang true inside me and what was not true. As time went on I began to question the pastor and church more and more. Things like, "If the bible says in the spirit of the Lord is liberty," why do we have all of these restrictive rules? "If the Bible says, Man was made in the image of God, male and female he created them and called their names Adam and Eve, why do they constantly refer to God as Him?" "If God's ways are above man's ways, then why does God get angry, and jealous?" "If the Bible says, God saw that everything he made was good, then why is man a sinner?"

The pastor's answers did not sit well with me. I left the church knowing that I would find the answers if I kept looking. I knew by now to seek and I will find.

More Soul Connections

What opened up for me was truly amazing. While living in NYC, I met a Korean man who called himself Charlie. Well, Charlie had organized a senior citizen group in the park to do yoga every morning at 7 am. I thought this was interesting. I learned about it from a senior citizen friend, a lady a lot older than me, who invited me to join them. I loved to hear the enthusiasm in her voice when she described how her health had gotten much better since attending Charlie's classes. Dorothy was her name, and she was insistent that I meet Charlie and come to his class.

Dorothy kept telling me, "You got to meet Charlie! I want you to come to this great class he has in the park." Of course, I went.

Charlie was humble and informative while he showed us *Dan Hak* yoga. This was a combination of yoga and *tai chi*. It also went beyond that. It was very enlightening, whereby he taught us about energy, and that this energy is everywhere and in everyone. He taught us how your mind is like a boat going down the stream and how we control this boat by our thoughts. We are to think positive to avoid ship wreck.

Also, the concept of *what I do to others I ultimately do to myself* was reintroduced into my thinking. I had heard this before in Catholic school as the golden rule, which teaches do unto others what I want done to myself; except Charlie explained it from the point of view that we are all connected in one spiritual body. It is like if I hurt my hand, my foot will feel it too.

Charlie taught me to hug trees to experience the energy of the tree. I tried it for the first time and it was true, I felt the energy from the tree myself. It was so wonderful! I suggest you try it sometime. It helps eliminate negative emotions.

One day, Charlie invited me to attend a session that was geared to meet your inner self. It sounded interesting. I decided to attend.

We all sat in a dimly lit room wearing loose, comfortable clothing. The instruction was given by Mya, the seminar leader. "You want to yell as loud as you can with the intention to meet your inner self. The entire focus of the exercise is to meet your inner self. You are going into dialog with your inner self. You do this as if your entire life depends on it." Mya stated with such depth and magnitude.

We all began with eager participation. The entire room had the thunderous, emotionally charged atmosphere similar to the Pentecostal church minus the music, as twenty participants from various walks of life and ages began bellowing out with screams of anticipation of meeting their inner selves. There were yells with such intensity that it seemed like it could stir up an earthquake.

All of a sudden, I had that same reconnection within myself that I had in the church that day. I was enraptured by a higher consciousness. I was aware of higher consciousness or awareness speaking through me. It began saying "You are loved, there is nothing to fear." I was amazed because all along I had been told that living according to a set of religious rules and dogma was the only way this experience can come through. But, here I was, not connected to any religious decree and was having the same spiritual connection.

I accepted this as my soul speaking. I grasped the reality that no religion, organization or way has a monopoly on this experience. The soul is my great companion. It is with me always. It is most apparent when the conscious mind is in the background. Any intensity, focus, concentration on communicating with it will bring it forward.

I have also participated in Native American Shaman ceremonies and have had the same spiritual soul connection. Something about being in intense heat and darkness, and engaged in prayer while being in a sweat lodge with other human beings, was a very expanding soul experience.

As I began to research more on soul connecting, I discovered different religions or ways of being had different methods to get in touch with the inner soul. There were the Whirling Dervishes who spin themselves in an ecstatic trance-like state to connect with the inner soul. The *Khamitian* rituals of ancient Egypt are also used to connect with one's inner Soul. While attending a *Khamitian* ceremony, I was surprised to hear the women, dressed in ceremonial white cotton dresses, speaking in tongues similar to what I heard myself speaking in church that day. The Siberian Shaman experience similar rituals. These types of rituals are also experienced in The *Bembe,* an Afro-Cuban ceremony which includes dance, drums and song.

In connecting with the soul, knock and the door will open. Use whatever method that provides a connection for you: whatever is in agreement with your heart for growth and development. If it opens your heart and nourishes your soul continue the path that works for you. This force within us asks for recognition. It is as necessary as drinking water to sustain the body. Communing with one's soul is like drinking from the spiritual fountain of life. It renews, it directs, it comforts and it is our intimate friend.

What I discovered next shifted my life forever. I discovered the soul is unconditioned, pure without judgments or limitations.

Love Without Limits

Humankind in his limited conscious has attempted to describe the All in All by human experiences. We can only describe something based on what we think we already know and understand, otherwise it is unknowable, *unless the unknowable reveals itself.* I observed that humankind colored experiencing the nature of the soul with dogma, religion and traditions. For, I had similar experiences in different spiritual and religious settings. My soul was communicating with me through all of those mediums. I found religions and other spiritual practices, dogma, and traditions were simply private interpretations of the soul's interaction.

Religions or ways of being are simply stories of ways the eternal may interact with temporal life. Human beings are redefining these stories every day. A cult is any religious story that says this is the only

147

way that a soul can interact with or come through the temporal. *For example the cult leader, or the pre-scribed dogma, teaches its practices without any room for questioning and exploring what is really so.*

In pursuing what is, one discovers that which is eternal. In the eternal, one can find the source of all, including happiness, healing, wealth, companion-ship, friendship, bliss and 'well rounded *beingness,* which is described as a fullness felt in the depths of one's being, a feeling, a wholeness. *(If there is such a word, if not I just created it like every other word.)*

I discovered that *beingness* can only be felt by connecting with that which is Eternal. The eternal is always sustained by what is true, meaning that it can answer all questions. The answer always benefits and sustains the cycle of life. It is these questions about life that seem to be invoked by the Soul. For the pur-suit of the Soul is to ultimately seek that which cre-ates or sustains its own growth through learning the art of *beingness.* It is lifted by happiness, and creativ-ity. Artists are a conduit for it. True expression also contains a glimpse of it. Celebrations and ceremonies are an acknowledgment of it. Sickness and sorrow is an initiation into it. It is ultimately, an encounter with our very own soul.

Note to Self: *As I monitor my thoughts to be more positive, I create a more positive and fulfilling life.*

Chapter 13:

The Complex Machine

We cannot deny that the human being is designed as a complex machine; meaning that we process food, air, water, thoughts and ways of being, as entirely automated functions, designed by a master designer.

Further, we humans are habitual creatures, who settle at times for what we hold to be sure, when in truth, we are clinging to an illusion. Just ask the wife who lost her husband at war. Or ask the marathon runners who experienced the explosion in Boston (2013). Ask Malaysian Airlines officials who lost contact with their plane filled with passengers (2014). What we cling to as *sure* may not be sure at all. Yet, we hold on to patterns of being or behaviors that we think will give us a particular outcome. We often accept that what we are convincingly told or taught will bring us the desired effect.

We need to understand, however, that energies

are always shifting. What was deemed an acceptable effect today will not guarantee an appropriate effect tomorrow. Energies at work are going to determine the outcome, and our energies are dynamically included in this mix.

Our Internal Power

At every moment of our lives we have the choice of how our energies are focused and how our day will go,

When I once mentioned this to a client, she said, "That is easy for you to say, but what about those who are incarcerated?"

I replied, "Consider that we humans usually treat our external experiences as if they have more weight than our internal experiences. When, really, our internal experiences are actually defining what is happening externally. The internal happenings are actually more important. A person can be imprisoned physically and choose to never be imprisoned mentally. We saw that example with the Great Nelson Mandela."

A person has true power when he can re-conceptualize the physical experience to make it beneficial. The same idea goes for sickness. That is my take on why the soul generates sickness in the first place. It is a way to re-contextualize the meaning being generated. Since our thoughts create our experiences. Why not create the very best story or outcome. Then put this perspective into action to have it mirrored in the physical.

When we live more consciously in everything

that we do, we become more present to life. Our actions are meant to have purpose, and to help us understand the spiritual laws behind the functioning of our bodies.

Seven Immutable Laws

As a result of the health challenges I have faced and conquered, I have come to understand seven immutable laws about the wonderful human body. I share them in the paragraphs that follow.

These immutable, or *unchanging* laws, stay the same throughout time. The body was not created to eat, but eating is used to help maintain this wonderful body machine. Everything that we do in or with our body machine exacts a cost or brings about a result. Think of your body as an ATM machine. It deals with actions like a withdrawals or deposits in a bank. Its costs are measured in vibrations, energy and lifeforce. To understand these laws is to understand the Divine Immutable Creator-

Immutable means: that which cannot be destroyed, or changed. There are natural, immutable laws of the body that are both seen and unseen parts of our design and make-up, but the key to healing and wellness lies mostly in the unseen. Understanding these laws and following them leads to health and wellness. Breaking these natural laws consistently tends to lead to dis-ease and non-wellbeing.

First Immutable law: This is the law of SELF-GENERATION, wherein each cell is made to reproduce after its kind. This means that the cells in your face will never reproduce and build the cells in your foot. Each cells has its own memory bank to reproduce after the cell it came from. This is a high intelligence to actually produce after its own kind. This will continue throughout the lifespan of the body. There is an unseen force – accessed through your very soul – that is the orchestrator of your cell's intelligence, and this is an automatic function that needs no input from you. The soul also has everything it needs to keep the entire body charged and able to regenerate.

Second immutable law: The law of CREATION OR DECAY: This law tells us that nothing is ever static; it is either creating or decaying. It is either building or tearing down. Every action is either reproducing or destroying the body, mind or soul. No one can destroy the spirit in the body, for it was never created as a separate entity, so it cannot be destroyed.

Third immutable law: This is the law of CONSTANT COMMUNICATION. This law acknowledges that the body is always interacting and communicating with every organ and cell, both outside and inside the body environment. Even when the body is asleep, communication is constant. Each communication is physical, chemical, magnetic, electrical, etheric or metaphysical.

Fourth immutable law: I call this the law of ACKOWLEDGEMENT. This law comes into play when there is neglect, for when the body's true expression is being ignored it begins to decline. We acknowledge this by taking time to listen to the body's language. What is the decline telling us? Then we need to re-confirm and re-align with why our body was made, and what we feel or know as our destined purpose upon this earth.

Fifth immutable law: This is the law of OUTWARD EXPRESSION, where the body serves as a mirror or outward expression of all inner thoughts. This is expressed in how we present our bodies, our physical demeanor, how we feel and our attitudes about our life. Our posture, our movements are body language and body communication.

Sixth immutable law: This is our INWARD EXPRESSION. These are our conversations or inner expression of our beliefs. *Challenge your beliefs because they will lead your life.* If the beliefs are not rooted in truth, one will not fulfill one's true intent, or our soul's purpose. *These* inward expressions dynamically affect our life force and wellbeing, so it is always wise to keep them on a high-vibrational level.

Seventh immutable law: This is the law of CREATIVITY, where our true passions in life can be fully expressed though our creative talents. Expression through creativity is our ultimate expression. Observe how energized you are when you create something fresh and new to do every day. It could be a new song, dance, writing, conversation, music, learning a new language, art or anything that gets your creative juices flowing. Creation puts you in the zone of full life flow. Enjoy it to the full!

These seven immutable laws are ways to use your body as a channel to access your destiny. Get and fulfill your true desires. Ensure that your desires impact not only yourself, but others in a positive and uplifting manner.

Realize that when you help people achieve what they want, you will also receive what you desire. Everyone is a reflection of you. Everything and everyone all comes from the One Source of all. Therefore, everything happens for a reason. We give thanks for all. *"We are not human beings experiencing spiritual lives, we are spiritual beings experiencing human lives." - Oprah Winfrey*

Subconscious Roots

The brain is like a computer. And, there is a conscious mind that runs the computer. Then there is a subconscious mind designed to run the conscious mind. Most of the choices we make are based on the subconscious choices we made about life's circumstances. If your life is not running the way you want it to run, then there could be a virus in the computer. This means you must reprogram the computer/brain by reprograming your subconscious and conscious minds.

How to Hack into the Subconscious

We run scripts which are words without meanings, but they help you reboot the subconscious programs that are running havoc in your life. We said earlier that all disease starts in the unseen, in the

154

subconscious first, so we request that you are diligent about observing what occurs in your life that affects your subconscious beliefs and thoughts. There is no such thing as an outside source causing your life. You create your reality from your beliefs.

Like a wise sower, look at what is growing around you in your life. If you are not happy there is a virus somewhere. We are here to access greater consciousness. We are here to experience fullness of joy, ease and greater enlightenment. This can be done by altering the subconscious mind, and eliminating those programs that block our free flow of high-vibrational thought.

Reprogramming is done through mediation, affirmations, vision boards, mantras and *hekaus* (which are words of power). These power words have absolutely no meaning, but are effective in accessing the deeper parts of our consciousness for connecting with our Source and for positive change.

Our subconscious gets programed with detrimental beliefs when we are young. For example, let's presume something uncomfortable happened to you when you were a child, and you made up something about it to deal with the experience. What you made up becomes lodged in your subconscious and becomes and acts like a gate keeper. Later, whenever you sense something similar may occur, your gate keeper subconsciously motivates you behave in a certain, defensive way to avoid recreating the event.

This, however, keeps you from being fully present with the issue at hand. This also blocks a free flow of energy in your life which causes missteps, disease, "bad luck" and misfortunes which bring down your energetic consciousness. You stop living life fully because you think you have seen, experienced or lived these circumstances before. This, of course, is not true, but if you believe it you continue on until you make what you believe true. This is what is meant by you become the creator of your reality and you become your own self-fulfilling prophet of your life and circumstances.

By stating power words that have no meaning you open up access points to greater consciousness. That is why the ancients would chant a mantra over and over that does not have any real meaning. They are sounds to allow greater access to the subconscious. Once the subconscious is accessed one then uses visualization with emotion to rewrite the program.

"Be brave enough to live life creatively. The creative is the place where no one else has ever been. You have to leave the city of your comfort and go into the wilderness of your intuition. You can't get there by bus, only by hard work and risk and not quite knowing what you are doing. What you'll discover will be wonderful. What you'll discover will be yourself." - Alan Alda

Note to Self: *look at working hard as being intently focused, committed and concentrated. Risk is being brave enough to act.*

Chapter 14:

Nourishing the Body

Foods are fuel and *foods are vibrations*. We will now focus on the physical factor and what we take in to our bodies.

Foods and Moods

Many so-called foods aren't really foods at all. Many are so laden with chemicals that they have a negative impact and can actually zap our energy and harm the very body we think we are feeding.

There is a strong correlation between the foods that we eat and our moods. Foods that are unnatural can make us feel depressed, sad, or ineffective and lacking focus. I often tell clients at chemicals can slow down the response time of getting your prayers answered. For, if our vibrations and thoughts are lack focus, our link-to-spirit broadcasting signal will be weak. If we are feasting on food-less foods, we are more prone to be feasting on negative thoughts and ideas, and also drawn to the company of negative people. This can actually slow down the receiving of your hearts desires.

A good way to remove low vibrational energy from the body is to fast and detox.

I once fasted for 21 days straight before. I once again began eating solid foods. I then ate veggies, fruits, juices and water for another 21 days. I noticed my thoughts became clearer, my prayers more focused, and my focused desire of moving to Jamaica became actualized within one month of completing the fast.

Fasting changes your vibrations. It cleanses the body and focuses the mind. If done correctly, it heals the body.

How to Fast

There are different types of fasting. Make sure you consult your health professional before choosing to fast. There are total abstinence fasts where nothing is consumed or drunk. There are partial fasts were only certain food or drinks are consumed. In these fasts it is important to hydrate yourself regularly with good quality water. Please read about what type of water to drink. I suggest alkaline water.

There are practitioners who recommend magnetized water or distilled water during a fast. It depends on why you are fasting. Seek the knowledge of a health practitioner to get more specific advice on how to tailor a fast for your individual needs, and how over what period of time is appropriate for optimum benefits.

You fast every time when sleeping. This gives the body time to rest, repair, and cleanse. Fasting strengthens our receptivity of thoughts and visualizations so they can actually seed our desires and physical manifestation of our dreams.

If you are new to fasting, and wish to embark on a 24-hour or longer fast, it is important to see a health specialist who understands fasting and how to properly break the fast when completed.

Prepare for fasting by focusing your mind on your purpose. There are several fasting books that explain where doctors were able to heal hypertension, diabetes, and other chronic illnesses by fasting. Total abstention of foods allows the body time to reconstruct and repair itself. Of course, it is very important to keep yourself hydrated. Apart from your fasting regimen, the rule is to drink half your weight in ounces of water every day. So if you weigh 150 pounds, divide your weight in half and that would be 75 ounces of water each day.

"I say to you some things only come by fasting and prayer." KJV Matt 17:21

Bad Love Affair

I used to love to eat spare ribs especially for the holidays. Ribs to me became like a bad love affair. When I would sit down to enjoy eating those tender ribs, fifteen minutes later, I would experience breaking out in hives. But, when served again, I would go back and eat them again, thinking that I gotten a bad stack the last time. I could sometimes even feel the room start spinning, or I would get downright nauseous. No matter who would cook them or when, I would eat them and end up not feeling well.

Yes, I really liked the taste, but when I evaluated it, pork ribs were not good for my body. If we become what we eat, then think about what the swine eats! No wonder I was getting nauseous! I was thinking, "Pork I love you," but the way it would treat me I know it did not love me!

Any animal meat, red meat or otherwise, especially if you're already sick with heart disease, cancer, or HIV, has been found to put considerable stress on the body! Anything dead cannot regenerate. It does not have the life giving properties needed for your body. It takes more energy to break down these types of foods. They are high cholesterol producing foods which only compound the health problem.

Begin to notice your body. Notice what gives you energy and what does not give you energy after eating. Energetic foods that are needed to heal, regenerate, and rebuild the body.

May I suggest keeping a food diary and jotting down how you feel after ingesting a certain food. If you know how to listen, your body will teach and show you what is good for you and what is not good for you. By observing what works and what does not work, you will become a scientist for the wellbeing of your own life. Then the next step is to follow that which empowers rather that which does not empower the body, mind and soul.

Then, from there, to be healthy and remain

healthy, stay away from energy draining foods. Move towards energy enhancing foods. Energetic foods regenerate the body.

Beware of energy foods that *slam* you after giving you an energy boost. These foods are notorious culprits like caffeine, and high sugar based foods. You want continuous energy. You will find it in consuming natural – not highly processed – foods.

High Octane Fuel for the Body

Fresh food, especially the importance of fresh organic fruits and vegetables, cannot be over stated in respect to its vital importance in the body temple. You will feel a boost of energy right away when you have eaten something that is good for you. Poor quality food will leave you feeling tired, sleepy and drained with a loss of productivity.

Natural foods – nature produced – like whole grains, nuts, fruits, and vegetables tend to be the best foods for the body. These foods are fuel to keep the body going. Take our cars, for example, if you continually put bad fuel in the gas tank, the car will eventually break down. Our bodies will break down, too, on a continuous diet of bad food. A lot of people feed their cars better than themselves, and are prematurely sleeping in the grave due to poor food and life choices. I wrote this book that your life may be full and happy.

Food Affects Your Thoughts

Body, mind and spirit all use food as a vehicle

for expression. The body expresses physically through the foods we ingest; the mind expressed emotionally what thoughts we accept. Spiritual expressions are shown by our actions. All are affected by food.

As a man thinks, so is he.

I am going to break this down for you. Remember *garbage in, garbage out.* Your body is the vessel for your thoughts. Your thoughts are affected by chemicals, food, drugs, and alcohol, with what you feed your mind. Your thoughts control your life. By giving your body low-nutrition foods you are also affecting the quality of your thoughts. Low nutrition equals low-quality thoughts. Just like when you put low octane gas in your car, it gives you lower gas mileage. It is the same with your food and the quality of your thoughts. The quality of your thoughts equals the quality of your LIFE!

How to Prevent Addiction and Obesity

Low quality foods are proven to cause cancer, diabetes, colon rectal problems, headaches, arthritis, genetic defects, fibromyalgia, irritability, muscle strain, arguments and discord. Also these FODS* (my coined name for Fake Foods) have in them addictive chemicals to make you want to eat more, causing disease and obesity. Obesity has been linked to a higher incidence of cancer and other debilitating diseases. Discernment is watching what we are sowing, so that we can understand what we are creating in life by our actions. The question is: Will we take care in what we are sowing so that we reap health and vitality – or will we reap sickness and disease? The choice is ours.

Foods that are *Loving*

I seek always to eat foods that pass the *'it loves me test'*. The *it loves me test* is when you eat a food and you notice shortly after eating it that you have an energy rush and during the day you still feel the positive effects of the food. Again, not like a sugar or caffeine high. These foods do not slam dunk you by making you feel high then dropping your energy to a real low! This dramatic energy swing is called the carbohydrate or 'carb crash' – after ingesting these types of foods you feel worse than before

The best way to eat is to eat little and live long off high nutritious foods. Choose foods that have the best nutritional value and respond favorably to the *it loves me test.*

Look for a combination of highly colorful foods. Take in all the natural colors of the rainbow. (Red, Orange, Yellow, Green, Blue, Indigo Blue-Purple, Violet.) These colors will make your dish more palatable and delicious. Not only are you taking in colorful, and beautiful foods, you are absorbing those energetic colors into your system. Each color resonates with an energy field and spectrum that connects to a particular organ and energy center of the body (chakra). See an earlier chapter.

I also try to avoid man made, genetically altered fruits and vegetables, especially barren fruits that don't have seeds in them. Why does man constantly think that he can improve on something that the Divine Creator made perfect? Fruits have seeds in them for a reason.

Fruits also spoil after a certain time for a reason, but not all natural fruits are quick to spoil, for some will last for months without spoiling. Eating chemically-treated fruits, to preserve a longer shelf life, is unnatural, and a big contributor to stomach indigestion and disease.

Genetically Modified Food Concerns

I am wondering about the effects of fruits with no seeds in them, they cannot produce after their own kind. Genetically Modified Foods (GMO) are foods that have been modified from their natural state. They will affect the body in ways we are yet discovering. Cancer, heart disease, obesity, and mental illnesses such as severe depression, are at an all-time high. Could it be from the types of foods we are ingesting? I will say *yes*. I believe this is playing a big part in promoting our modern diseases. Our ancestors' diet was not filled with GMO's, artificial foods and chemicals. They didn't have the obesity, cardiovascular problems, and diabetes that plague people today.

I suggest eating fruits that are organic and that have seeds, and avoid genetically modified foods. Nature is intelligent. Divine Nature created fruits and vegetables the way it did for a reason. Man thinks he is more intelligent than Divine Nature which created him. This is an arrogance that can be costly to human life.

Ari Levaux wrote a great article for the Atlantic magazine, January 9, 2012, titled *"The Very Real Dangers of Genetically Modified Foods."* The article informs us that when we consume GMO foods we are ingesting more than proteins, and vitamins. We are also ingesting information. Information which can alter the way the body functions.

Can this information shut down certain functioning in the body? According to a study out of China, documented in the *Cell Research Journal* by Lin Zhang in 2011, it does just that. It can stop certain cellular function by actually reprogramming the way the body performs certain liver functions.

This, in turn, can cause cancer. Man in his arrogance thinks he can improve nature. He has created barren genetically dead fruits and vegetables without fully understanding the dangers of it.

In Europe and some U.S. states, laws have be passed for mandatory labeling of GMO foods. Some places have banned these foods all together. Why is cancer so high in the US? Is it because we are ingesting foods that are artificial or not genetically alive?

What is dangerous or harmful in eating foods the way nature intended? It is something to consider and think about. I certainly advocate proper labeling of these GMO foods. I want to know what kind of corn, rice, potatoes, soy, and fruits I am ingesting. There is a long list. Support Farmer's Markets and if you can grow your own foods. Your life and family's life may depend on it. If this book is banned you can guess why.

Basic Herbs

Herbs are for the healing of the nations, the scriptures tell us. I have used herbs throughout the years with great success. Also, I am an herbalist. I have studied herbs in different countries in order to understand their application and usage. Here is a list of key herbs with their wonderful healing properties:

SUPPORTIVE HERBS:

Ginger: strengthens digestion; an anti-aging supportive herb.

Lemongrass: eliminates excess mucous and gas in the body.

Bay leaf, thyme, garlic, chamomile: all calm the nerves.

Sarsaparilla: cleans the blood.

Rosemary; provides immune support.

Myrrh: cleans the blood.

Cascara Segrada: cleans the intestines.

Horsetail: strengthens bones and hair.

Ginseng: increase energy.

Fo Ti: a liver and kidney tonic.

Burdock: a blood cleanser.

Yellow Dock: strengthens the liver; helps with digestion.

Water: I suggest 'Fiji' water, Jamaican Catherine springs water, coconut water, and alkaline water, reverse osmosis water, magnetic water.

The above list is all "nature created." There is an inherited wisdom in eating foods that were created by the same force that created us.

When we are over-laden with scores of artificial foods, and chemicals we are denaturing our bodies. Our organs have to work twice as hard to use unnatural foods. That stresses the organs to the point where they begin to break down.

Do you think a peanut butter sandwich will work in a CD player? Certainly not. And although this is a dramatic correlation, this is what happens to your body over time when you continuously feed the body unnatural foods. The body will not work effectively. The body was not designed for artificial foods. Like the CD player was not designed for peanut butter sandwiches.

Personal Choices

The body handles foods better in small little portions throughout the day. Let it be not artificial food, chemical foods, and fried foods, high cholesterol foods, or foods that are too rich or too spicy. Do let it be a lot of organic fresh fruits and veggies! I feel there will be a future time when we will get back to basics like nature intended. Possibly no meat eating at all! We are aiding the planet when we are vegetarian.

This has to be a personal choice. Less land space and water resources are used to grown vegetables and fruits than cultivating animals for slaughter. We are saving our bodies. We don't have to eat meat to get protein. My daughter was a vegetarian from age 6 to 12 years at that time she did not eat any meat, or milk or eggs or cheese. She was never sick during those years. Vegetarians, overall, are healthier than carnivores. Studies have proven that they have balanced blood pressure, less incidence of heart disease, better weight management, less incidence of sugar diabetes, less incidence of osteoporosis, less incidence of Alzheimer's disease and other maladies. According to Michael F. Roisen MD, author of *The Real Diet: Make Yourself Younger with What You Eat,* "People who consume saturated, four-legged fat have a shorter life span and more disability at the end of their lives. Animal products clog arteries, zap your energy and slow down your immune system.

However, the best way to find out what is best for you is to become your own observer. Notice what makes you feel good and what does not. Make a pact with yourself to follow those practices that gives you optimal functioning. I know persons who feel they cannot live without eating meat. I also know people who feel they cannot live without drinking alcohol and smoking tobacco. Are these things the best for the body? These items can be addictive.

Why Suffer?

Your body always gives you choices. There will even be a choice if one day you wind up in a hospital for detrimental food or lifestyle choices. I observed this as a hospitals nurse for many years. I saw the *'sufferation'* of people with diseases, and I would always ask my patients, "What happened to you? What caused you to get this way?" I took note of their answers and discovered particular patterns in behavior and thoughts that came before the illness began.

The body really does rebel after giving it too

much garbage food. Garbage in, garbage out! Socrates once said, "Let your food be your medicine and your medicine be your food." You will feel and look much better. Your thoughts and skin will become clearer. You will have more energy, for sure.

This is the approach I took with myself and many of my patients. I saw great responses with the improvement of my health and that of patients who chose to follow my guidance. Their health turned around after changing what they consumed.

Remember no one knows your body better than you. Again, observe how you feel after you eat something. Notice if it gives you energy or take away your energy. If it takes away your energy, chances are your body is telling you it does not like it.

If you are energized and you stay that way, keep that food choice on your list. I like chocolate, milk chocolate and lots of it. So one summer night I walked to my favorite ice cream store for a nice, big, cup of chocolate ice cream. I ate it all with great satisfaction, carefully scraping the sides of the bowl, yummy! I felt high as the sugar and chocolate explosion coursed in my veins. Soon after, I was very tired-unusually tired so I decided to go to bed. I woke up the next day with what was called a sugar and chocolate hangover! I had no energy and was tired all morning, feeling like somebody had beaten me up. It did not pass the *it loves me test*. Observation is the greatest teacher of what works best for your body.

Note to Self: Life is about making loving choices to sustain higher quality of being.

Energy Vampires

Just like there are foods that drain us, there are people in our lives that can drain us energetically as well. I call them energy vampires. They rob us of our creative and productive power. Be aware of how you feel when you are around others. Some will uplift you, others will rob you of your energy.

Remember, energy is subtle. It is something that we cannot see, but we can feel. Energy vampires don't always know they are vampires, but some are certainly aware that their actions and words are pulling you down. It often makes them feel good or superior to see you energetically down.

But if you are left feeling depleted, you don't have to stay that way. Just breathe in and center yourself, then call upon Divine Energy and put a protective, energetic shield of white-violet light around you. Smile within and be more selective in your dealings with energy vampires in the future.

Note to Self: Remember this rule when around people: energy gain stay around, energy drain leave alone.

Chapter 15:

Earth: The 3-D Hologram

How does the Creator express life in this world? Life is expressed through the *seen*, and especially through physical bodies. The body is the Creator's third dimensional vehicle for expressing Divine Spirit for all to see.

The Creator experiences the third dimension on this Earth – sometimes called a 3-D hologram – through 3-D life forces. This life force includes the energy of human beings. Your living body is the life-force vehicle that the Creator uses to experience this earth plane through you. Sound complicated?

It isn't. This simply means that the Creator experiences our world through us and other life forms. The Creator is *All-In-All*.

Spirit supplies life for the body; the body supplies the mouth, and the mouth is intended to speak Source Energy's Divine will into this world. Out of the mouth, faith is express to the world. By hearing the Creator's word, our vibrational frequencies and physical make-up is changed.

Faith comes by hearing wisdom from others, and hearing our own inner voice from the Source. Our third dimensional vehicle, our body, has a purpose, and it is wisdom to know how to respond to it.

To make it function at the optimal level there are rules and guidelines about what to put into it to make it work better; when to eat and when not to eat; when to sleep and when not to sleep. The body is an amazing machine. It is made by wisdom and it was brought into being through by the word of the Creator (another word for source energy that means Mother-Father Creator).

We are Source Energy expressed in human form. *"We are here not to condemn or bring judgment, only to enlighten and set free." KJV Mat 7:1, Luke 6:37 Know the truth and the truth shall set you free!*

Note to Self: Everything has a purpose!

There is a reason for everything! There are no accidents in this world. Everything is created and orchestrated by Divine thoughts, wisdom, actions, and words. Look beyond what you see and feel what is there.

Clear Perspective

I met a woman in New York, her name was Kathy, and she shared with me her secrete for success. She said, "Life to me is 10 percent of what actually happens and 90 percent how I interpret it!"

I thought wow! It made me feel that I have a choice as to how I respond to day to day activities and life. I felt better when I changed my perceptions to my inner control, rather than allowing outer circumstances to have control over me. I found gratitude was a great help in allowing me to take back control over my own life. I also began to realize that all things happen for a reason, and that trusting the Creator's plan for the unfolding of my life was truly perfect.

Note to Self: Think of all the physical blessings you have/own and what you have been able to accomplish so far.

The Perfect Inner Clock

The body has its own internal clock. It sends signals when to sleep, when to eat, when to wake, etc. It is regulated by hormones and the body's internal functions.

It is important to follow your body's internal system. It is important not to eat when it is time to sleep. After the sun goes down, your body begins to prepare itself for sleep. It is the body's internal clock not to eat when it is time to sleep. Eating at this time can prevent food from digesting properly and has been known to cause headaches, excess weight gain, constipation, and nightmares.

Upon awakening, this time is best suited for affirmations and prayers. Deep breathing to oxygenate the body to get it going is very crucial. Set the day's intention: What do you intend to have happen today?

Pursuit of the Soul

Ask for it, see yourself accomplishing it. This is also a great time for reprogramming your subconscious, since at this time of awakening and before sleep the subconscious is at the optimum time for reprogramming.

Cultivating our Spirit, Finding our Joy

Understand how your mind works, and it will give you greater access to a great and fulfilling life. It is like having abilities shown in the movie "Limitless." Instead of using a synthetic drug to give you greater access to your consciousness, you will use methods of cultivating your spirit.

We are here on earth to cultivate our spirit, for this is the real *pursuit of the soul*. We are here to raise consciousness. We are here to grow, to experience the fullness of joy and the abundance of life. Be in the flow of times and seasons of the body, for it is connected to the universe.

Seasons and Cycles

Every heavenly body has a season and a flow when it is at its optimal peak. Each organ has its optimal time to regenerate. Use the following chart to determine the optimum regenerating time in each 24-hour period. Paying attention to this 'timing' can bring balance to each organ that needs respite or attention. Everything in nature is ruled by cycles. Get in rhythm and harmony with each cycle and you will be more in balance. Timing is of critical importance.

174

There are times when each organ cycles for internal cleansing, or for taking of supplements, or for ideally making affirmations for that particular organ.

When taking supplements, food or fluids to balance a particular organ, it will be have its greatest effect if taken during the time that organ is in its cycle. For instance, if stomach issues are present, one would take herbs or foods or fluids that balance the stomach between the hours of 7 am and 9 am.

Gallbladder ....11 pm - 1 am
Liver .... 1 am - 3 am
Lung .... 3 am - 5 am
Large Intestine .... 5 am - 7 am
Stomach ....7 am - 9 am
Spleen ....9 am - 11 am
Heart ....11 am - 1 pm
Small Intestine ....1 pm - 3 pm
Bladder ....3 pm - 5 pm
Kidney ....5 pm - 7 pm
Sex Organs ....7 pm - 9 pm
Thyroid/Adrenal ....9 pm - 11 pm

For more details on this subject see a qualified health professional, holistic health practitioner, acupuncturist, Chinese medicine practitioner, Chi-Gong practitioner, etc., who has knowledge of this topic.

Note to Self: *Whatever intention I focus on is a request to the Universe.*

Energetic Cycles

Try to function without breathing. We can't. Nothing is ever accomplished without the breath; and it is important to breathe deeply, whether working, playing or resting.

I found the best time to exercise the body is in the morning, when the body is at an optimal level to accomplish physical tasks. Our energy correlates with the sun. When the sun rises, our energy arises to accomplish the tasks at hand. As the sun goes down, so does our physical energy. Source Energy designed it that way.

It is best to do all your physical work in the day. Do your mental, thinking, and meditative tasks in the evening. It is best to rest or sleep at night. This is in harmony with the natural cycle. Every twenty- eight days is a new month or cycle. There are actually 13 months to a year instead of the 12 months in the Gregorian calendar.

According to the Old Farmer's Almanac, there are times and cycles when to plant food and when not to plant food. This almanac shows the cycle of the moon in the months for every twenty-eight days. A woman's natural menstrual cycle is average of twenty-eight days. We recommend aligning yourself with this natural time calendar.

Manifest Your Inner Desires

We are the ever- present generators of all creative thought on the Earth.

The Living Creator's energy lives and moves within us. It moves as vibrations to stir our own innate energy and our desires to create and co-create with the universe. We have a longing to manifest our inner desires.

This begins through the transformation of the self, the learning of our true purpose. We each have an individual purpose as to why we are here. We humans have a common purpose, but we also have an individual purpose. No one can accomplish our individual purpose but our self.

A wise woman once said: "If you choose not to accomplish your purpose it will be lost throughout all time. Your purpose is unique to you."

No one here can do what we are here to do. Being a co-creator with this living divine energy; shows that we are made in the very image of the Source. All things are possible when we come to understand this truth.

Vibrational Awareness

A healthy body is dependent upon — and reflects — healthy, energetic vibrations in its organs. The following chart correlates the emotional vibrations with the responsive organs.

Emotional thought vibrations	Affected Organ
Love: one of the highest thought vibrations.	(+) All body systems
Peace: inner calmness of mind, body and spirit.	(+) Nervous System

Joy: inner resonance of happiness.	(+)The Spleen, Pancreas
Faith: trust in knowing that all will be well.	(+)The Pituitary Gland
Bliss: inner good feeling of being present.	(+) Pinal Gland
Gratitude: inner thankfulness and appreciation.	(+) Lungs
Ecstasy: inner connection to Source Energy.	(+) Reproductive Organs
Passion: inner moving to create with vigor	(+) Heart
Enthusiasm: inner excitement - connection to Source Energy.	(+) Heart
Positive Belief: inner confidence about one's thoughts.	(+) Endocrine system
Happiness: outer expression of joy.	(+) Heart
Contentment: outer expression of being present.	(+) Bones
Apathy: outer expression of being hopeless.	(-) Bones
Boredom: outer expression of not knowing one's purpose.	(-) Cerebellum
Frustration: inner expression of not expressing one's goals.	(-) Heart (-) Pancreas
Overwhelmed: inner expression of not expressing faith and belief in one's abilities.	(-) Lungs
Negative Belief: lack of confidence in one's thoughts.	(-) Limbic System
Disappointment: judgment of one's missing a goal or purpose.	(-) The Lungs

Doubt: an inner lack of faith that is introduced in one's thoughts.	(-) The Pituitary
Worry: a pressing, consistent lack of faith in one's outcome	(-) The Adrenal Gland
Blame: an outer expression of directing one' outcome on another or situation.	(-) The Thymus Gland
Anger: an inner expression of judgment based on wanting and needing change for control.	(-) The Liver
Rage: an outer expression of out of control anger.	(-) The Gallbladder
Revenge: an outer expression of judgment based on hatred of what is present or occurring.	(-) The Heart
Jealously: an inner expression of what you see has power and love higher and greater than one's self.	(-) The Ocular Nerves
Guilt: an inner judgment of one's self of being wrong.	(-) The Liver, (-) The Kidneys, (-) The Skin
Unworthiness: an inner expression of low self-esteem.	(-) The circulatory System
Depression: inner expression of anger turned on one's self.	(-) Central Nervous System, The Spleen
Fear: inner expression of not knowing one's self or power of being in the present.	(-) The Kidneys

The Creation Formula

Here is the formula for creation. It is a very

simple formula. This is how it works: Thoughts become words, words become actions, actions shape the world. Therefore, thoughts become things.

Whatever it is that you wish create it begins with this formula.

The translation of words into actions is where we need to put creative energy to work. Call on intuition; call on source energy; call on affirmations, and call on visualization to muster all your strength.

Stay focused and do not give up and your desires will birth into reality.

Through this process we get to know ourselves. We know what we are capable of and that is the greatest love and magnificence of all!

Focus on the outcome; focus on the steps to get there. Most importantly, have fun, faith, thanks and praise for the journey of it all.

Note to Self: If it is to be… it is up to me!

Chapter 16:

Keys for Wise Living

If we have eyes to see, we will see that the Creator has given us more than just life, the Creator has placed within us the wisdom to live that life to the full. This wisdom, of course, must be sought out and practiced as an integral part of our thinking and beliefs, as we deal with life on a daily basis.

Giving Back to Our Creator

The greatest gift one can give the Creator for life and wisdom is to have lived a happy and fulfilled life. So, when everything seems to be going haywire and crazy around you, do not despair. You are being tested. You are getting ready to put wisdom to work and elevate to the next level. Be encouraged! Use the tool of wisdom in its many applications. Use forgiveness. Use gratitude. Visualize your life the way you desire it to be. Affirm positive and loving statements for yourself. Keep pushing forward beyond your challenges, knowing that this too shall pass!

All parents want their children to be happy. This is a great gift. The Creator wants us to be happy. It is our divine right; but there are tests and challenges. So sharpen your sword and gear up to fight for your happiness. The real battle always happens within. Go within and win the battle, using wisdom.

Keys for Wise Living

I discovered there are key principles of wisdom that, if we choose to live by them, will insure that our lives will be happier, more productive, and make more sense no matter what the challenges may be.

These key principles of wise living are as follows:

1. Everything is energy: We are here on earth because we were designed energetically to be here. Appreciate energy by learning what to do to preserve and generate your personal energy. You will have more clarity, focus and solid health as a result. This has been studied and researched by the Chinese since before 2400 B.C. Through cultivating one's natural energy flow, it was discovered a person was able to slow down degeneration of the body, gaining greater health and a longer life span.

2. Infinite intelligence: There is an infinite intelligence energy field that connects with our energy field. It sustains us. This intelligent energy field is called by many names, but all refer to God or Creator. This Divine energy mutually supports us and our focused efforts. One of our focused efforts is called prayer. Prayer is embraced in many cultures and religions. All have believers who confirm their prayers or focused intentions have been answered by infinite intelligence. What you believe you must receive.

3. Love is unconditional: Love is not complete if there are conditions. Love yourself unconditionally, and you will be able to love others in the same way, completely, without reservations.

4. Passion is necessary: The emotion of passion is essential if we are to accomplish our life's mission on this earth. No passion, no movement toward our goals.

5. Focus: Whatever you focus on, that is what you will attract.

6. Believing is creating: You must attract what you believe. Life, on every level, confirms *as you believe it is*. If you believe the world is unfair, it will continue to show up in your life as unfair. If you believe all men are no good. You will continue to draw men into your life which will meet your criteria of *no good*. If you subconsciously believe you are a second class citizen you will show up that way. Self-reflection is a powerful way to observe how you show up in the world through your beliefs. If a man has a poverty consciousness, no matter how much money he is given he will always end up poor.

7. Abundance is our natural state: We are here to live and align ourselves with the natural order of abundance. Once this truth is grasped, one will never lack to have his or her needs fulfilled.

8. Everything happens for a reason: There are no accidents. Energy in motion, including your own, determines exactly what happens.

9. No victims: This statement may be hard to accept. There are no victims, for we on either a conscious level or an unconscious level create our reality. Once we take full accountability for the way our life is going, we can then put ourselves in the driver's seat to do something about it.

10. Learning to be non-judgmental: We are here to practice non-judgment of ourselves and others. Whatever we dislike about others is what we dislike about ourselves.

11. Race is an illusion: There is no such thing as a white person. There is no such thing as a black person. All human kind come from the same hue of brown. Add more light to brown, and it becomes beige. Add darker shades to brown, and it becomes dark brown. Then there is every shade in between. By redefining who you are, you redefine yourself by experiences rather than race, wealth, heritage or status.

12. Be true to yourself. Follow what is in your heart or you will never find the joy you seek. Your external life is shaped by your desires within.

Note to Self: Wear wisdom is a rare and precious jewel.

Chapter 17:

Living as an Open Bloom

Get ready and raise up. You can heal and change your life. You can bloom as a flower!

Through the struggles, through the pain in life, lift up your thoughts and choose to love and care for yourself. It is a conversation and choice we all have to make for ourselves. In short, we must grasp the concepts and practices that allow us to open and bloom!

Practices for a Higher Vibrational Life

Here, now, are practices and insights for keeping the body mind and soul fit and productive – for *blooming on a daily basis*. Observing these precepts will insure positive results; while continuously ignoring them will invite the undesirable.

1. Breathe deeply everyday: Be conscious of

your breath, your feelings, and your life. Deep breathing is the key to having and producing flow in your life. This is where you can truly feel what you are accomplishing. Deep breathing cleanses the body's organs, sets your mind straight and frees it from negative emotions.

The breath connects us all. As I am breathing out air, you are taking it in. As you are releasing air, I am taking it in. We all share this space where we share the breath. We are vibrational, energetic, and electrical beings. By breathing in, we take in particles of the atmosphere that have been charged with living matter since this planet began. We also take in energy dust and matter from other planets and universes. We then charge this air with our own energy and vibrations and release it out for someone else to interpret.

Consciously deep breathe fresh air for at least five minutes a day. Breathing increases our vitality and strength. It increases the oxygen content to our cells, and our cells use it as fuel. Breathing gives our brain functionality. It eliminates toxins from our bodies. It cleanses our lungs. It gives us energy. It converts foods into fuel. A great way to breathe deeply is by singing to yourself. (Singing is discussed below.)

Remember to breathe deeply from your diaphragm. Expand your lungs as much as possible and release out deeply and slowly. Repeat and continue for five minutes. This is a great pick-me-up for the early mornings. This increased oxygen you are breathing in will give you an energetic boost.

Deep breathing, however, is conscious breathing. Think about breathing; it is mindful breathing.

Try this *Breath Mediation: Imagine the person-ified breath is speaking to you. Close your eyes and connect into your inner being. Hear the words, "I am the person leading you, I am your breath, and I am the invisible. I am the creator of your life. Use me to create your life as a driver uses the car to get to his destina-tion. Go to the beautiful spaces in your life and breathe it in, breathe in that vibration." Then notice how you feel. Be with this feeling. Let it direct your life.*

2. Exercise to condition body and mind: It strengthens the body, and cleanses the blood. It cleanses the lymphatic system. It allows oxygen to permeate all the cells. Exercise also raises your vibra-tion. It is hard to be depressed when your body is mov-ing and releasing pent-up energy through exercising. Exercises such as brisk walking, swimming, aerobics, dancing, bike riding, cleaning house, and yoga, are all very effective for your body and mind.

Yoga means the joining of mind and spirit to-gether. This stretches and conditions the body and mind. Yoga practice is over 2000 years old. It is taught extensively in India, and is very popular now in the U.S. The benefits and studies of yoga practice are too numerous to list here. I encourage you to try it.

Physical exercise raises your vibration and puts you in touch with your body. It is another partner that helps you, like the breath, to be a vibrant being.

3. Water elevates your emotions: Drink wa-ter, alkaline water. It cleanses the body, restores the body's natural functions and keeps you high vibra-tional. When you are high vibrational you can mani-fest your desires easier.

Water is amazing! We bathe in it, shower with it, swim in it, drink it, and immerse ourselves in it for fun and play! Raise your emotions also by washing dishes, washing your clothes or the floor, for water is the universal solvent.

When we water the body on the inside as we drink, we replenish its' natural state. Scientists state that we are 75%-90% water composition, perhaps even more. This water constantly needs to be replaced. Water keeps our organs happy and healthy. It cleanses the blood and flushes out impurities. I think water is one of the Creator's best inventions, especially when I am in warm tropical waters, floating ever so buoyantly.

Water is very healing. It has the power to shift moods, de-stress the body, eliminate negative feelings, clean the skin, and re-mineralize the body when bathed in minerals or mineral water. Many natural healers use herbal baths to eliminate negative vibes and disease from their patients with excellent results. Contact with water is an essential part of living.

I found the best waters to drink are spring water, alkaline, or distilled water, depending on your objective. Avoid city pipe water for drinking purposes it is filled with sediment and debris from the pipe. If you must use it, get a good home water filter. The best water filter that I found is an alkaline water filter. This will help in eliminating the debris. This debris can clog your blood vessels and cause damage to the brain and over time can poison the body.

Make sure your home water filter eliminates chlorine, mercury, and arsenic. These chemicals have been found to cause nerve damage and psychological problems. It is healthy for the body if your filter makes the water alkaline rather than keeping it acidic. You can get a PH tester to check your water to see if it is acid or alkaline. Alkaline water is best for the body, for it pulls debris and toxins out of the body. You feel better and it helps with muscle tone.

Not drinking enough water can cause diseases like kidney malfunction, diabetes, spleen malfunction, liver dis-ease, heart failure and skin eruptions.

If you have bad skin with a lot of acne and skin problems, you may not be drinking enough of the best water. Water flushes toxins out of the large and small intestines. If toxins are building up in your system, this can affect the skin and other organs. Water makes the organs work better. It is essential in eliminating toxins and cleansing the blood. Water keeps the body flowing and the body's vibes harmonious. Vegetables and fruits are high water foods. That helps the body replenish water that is lost during the day. This also helps to postpone unnecessary aging of the body.

See my book *"Beautyflow"* TM on vibrational beauty and anti-aging. It goes into more detail on a vibrational beauty regime that has practical day to day practices that keep the body, mind and spirit in balance.

4. Listen to feel-good music and sing: Sing to yourself feel-good songs everyday first thing upon arising. Music is a powerful shifter of vibrations. When listing to music or singing notice how it makes you feel. Singing to yourself releases endorphins from the brain and it picks up your moods and causes you to breathe deeper than you normally would. Singing your daily affirmations is great. If you feel energized it is a good vibe song. If you feel sad or despondent change the music. Sing a happy song and you will be happy. When you are happy it raises your immune system and assists your thoughts to become more creative.

There has been much research into the effects of music. Music programs the subconscious mind. The more violent and negative lyrics one listens to, the lower vibrational and violent one becomes. The positive and loving music and lyrics one listens to the higher vibrational one becomes. We have seen the upsurge of violence in our society as music has become more violent and disrespectful to life. Music programs your vibrations, for music is sound and sound affects all vibrational creatures that move with rhythm. The question is "Do you like the rhythm of your life?"

Change your sounds, change your life; change your life, change your destiny. Change the vibrations you listen to. For violence brings more violence. Love brings more love. Make your life and surroundings harmonious, and your surroundings will reflect this inside and out.

Note to Self: LALALA... LA means I love you!

5. Eat high-vibes foods: Eat veggies, fruits and herbs, organic if possible. This assists the body in connecting to high vibrations. Natural live food contains high vibrations. I have gone into greater detail on this subject elsewhere in this book.

6. Sleep is healing: Human beings spend about a third of their lives sleeping. It is important to get the right amount of sleep for the body. Sleeping changes your brainwave activity, which is essential for nerve repair. In times past, it was thought that sleep was a wasteful activity, but in fact it is time well spent. It actually can assist a person to be more productive during waking hours. Beethoven created the fifth symphony from his dreams. Many cures from aliments were discovered through dreams. During this sleep cycle the body is able to contact the deeper elements to receive information. In the creative jungles of thought, while asleep, one becomes more magnetic. This magnetism attracts what you focus on the most.

Speaking of magnetism, magnetic mattresses are great for sleeping and relieving pain. Rather than trying artificial sleep enhancers, I suggest you try using a magnetic mattress. It helps with reaching deeper states of consciousness, while relieving pain and over tiredness. For a peaceful sleep, make sure the room temperature is comfortable, not too hot or not too cold. It is important to sleep in a comfortable bed. Sleeping with the radio or TV on disrupts sound sleep, and can over time adversely affect your health.

Sleep in loose, comfortable clothing. Avoid sleeping in bra, jock straps, and briefs so the blood circulation can reach throughout the body easier.

Keep a journal to write your dreams down when you awake. Who knows, perhaps the next cure for a disease or a creative invention is waiting inside you. Are you unable to dream? Practice meditation, as it assist you in accessing the deeper states of mind to awaken your dream world.

One additional thought. I believe it wise to take a day of rest, to refresh the mind and get some extra sleep. I believe in resting on Saturday. That is sundown Friday to sundown Saturday.

7. Commune with Source energy: Source is often called God, The Creator, or the Universal Oneness. Commune through meditation and/or prayer. Mediation is a very old and proven technique that calms the mind, strengthens the immune system and heals the body. Prayer is communication with source energy. Prayer is an opportunity to show gratitude for the marvelous creation that we are.

When you allow yourself to connect with Source energy, you are staying in balance. You continue to be a channel for the Divine. When you are a channel for the Divine, your creativity and your strength are renewed. Your harmonics are raised.

Note to Self: Gratitude is one of the master keys for a happy life.

8. Spoken affirmations: Speak and energize the atmosphere with your words. Imprint your desires to the universe. Words create your world. Affirmations allow the law of attraction to activate in your space. See my reference to Dr. Emoto's book- "The Hidden Messages in Water." Understand how words affect water and humans. We are mostly water. Words and sounds have an effect on water. (More on this in the next chapter.)

9. Relate to positive and uplifting people: I had this experience when I met Stevie Wonder for the first time. I was modeling for an African designer in NYC, and decided to take in a Stevie Wonder live performance. I walked up to him after the show and greeted him. He was smiling. He greeted me back. I noticed being in his space that I felt a lot of love and acceptance. Stevie did not let his blindness stop him from enjoying life.

It was as though he had received extra sensors to compensate for his physical blindness. I saw him for what he was without him having to tell me. This good feeling or vibration remained with me for two days. I noticed that his presence and being were not a result of what he said, but from the vibrations he was emanating.

When you believe and know who you are, this emanates forth from your energy field. It identifies the real you, no matter what culture or status. I found one does not have to profess who they are; it is one's being that shines forth.

Who do you feel that you are? The answer isn't found in thinking who you are; nor by others telling you who you are. So, who are you really?

I say, we are all magnificent beings of light, with creative power, thoughts and wisdom. We can have whatever is it that we wish. It is being focused and staying with that higher vibration that draws our wishes to us. Be committed to practicing these concepts for 30 days, and you will feel a shift in your energy vibration. You will become a magnet for attracting what it is that you desire.

10. Keep a journal: Take time each day to write down your goals and accomplishments. Go back and read your comments when you need a jolt or a reminder of who you are.

11. Choose uplifting entertainment: Select movies, audio messages, music, books that makes you feel good, not sad or depressed.

12. Enjoy nature: Plan some time for being in peaceful, beautiful scenic places in nature. You'll feel tranquility and peace of mind. Trees and lots of vibrant green foliage also have a high degree of negative ions that help oxygenate the body.

13. Laugh often: There are three things that bring us in unison with the Creator: a big belly laugh is one of them. It releases endorphins and it makes you feel good and releases stress.

14. Be creative: Let your creativity flow. It is a way of releasing judgment of yourself. Allow yourself to express who you are through creating something like art, pottery, sewing, designing, writing, cooking, etc.

15. Play with children: Learn to connect with your inner child. Go back in time and remember when you had no responsibilities; you were carefree without worries. Playing with children allows you to be free of adult stresses. Connect with inner child energy and be free again.

16. Practice being loving: Show love to yourself and others. This will raise your vibrations. When you feel good, you and everyone around you benefits.

17. Let you passions show: Reaching your goals and dreams is possible only with a healthy stirring of passion. Being excited and enthusiastic is contagious! Don't be afraid to let your passions show, and flow!

18. Enjoy the sunshine: Experience the healing energies of the sun for at least a few minutes a day. Eating fruits and vegetables is eating converted sun fuel, and the chemical makeup of the body is affected in a positive way. The sun purifies, so it is burning off the artificial 'stuff' inside of you. An anti-sun philosophy is unnatural. We need to get as much sunlight as we can tolerate, but use wisdom in taking the sun in small doses until we get used to it.

The sun affects our moods and keeps us feeling younger. People actually can get depressed without sunlight. This is called 'SAD' or seasonal affective disorder. It is a depression brought on from a lack of sunlight and changes brought on from our diets. The sun gives us subtle information through the sun rays to uplift, encourage, and stabilize our moods. It also helps to heal thyroid disorders and certain types of Cancer. It regulates the thyroid and hormones.

Sunlight is great for interacting with *melanin*. Everyone has melanin in varying degrees. It is a natural hormone in our bodies. Melanin is what gives us our pigmentation in our skin. We get darker by increasing our melanin hormones. If we did not have any melanin we would die. The sun sends to our melanin droplets of information to grow and stay healthy. Melanin is like an extra brain. It receives the sun's information and allows our bodies to absorb the sunlight. Sunlight produces vitamin D.

Vitamin D makes our bones stronger. I also believe the sun gives us other nutrients that scientist have not discovered yet. The sun has the power to grow all the fruits and vegetables that we eat. The sun's energy converts a tiny seed, with rain and soil, into food. The Creator gave us the sun to make food, and food gives us fuel for our bodies.

The use of sunscreen is promoted to prevent skin cancer. Sunscreen is made up of a variety of chemicals. If you must use sunscreen, use sunflower oil with zinc oxide. This is a natural sunscreen.

Sunshine is excellent for healing dis-eases. Sun bathing gives us *phyto*-nutrients from the sun. Sunlight gives us information from the sun; but always use wisdom in the amount of exposure to the sun's rays.

19. Live a balanced life: Eat, pray, work and play. These are balanced aspects of a healthy lifestyle. If you feel your life is like a treadmill, take a look at your heart inventory. Are you balancing your life? Review all the points listed in this chapter, and you will be reminded as to how to practice balance with positive results and wellbeing.

20. Thoughts of love and healing: I encourage you to send and receive healing and loving thoughts. This keeps you in loving and raised vibrations. Your vibration channel will stay on the love station. What you reflection is what you will receive.

21. Remember your ancestors: Respect their ancestral wisdom and ask for their guidance. Tune into these inner guides, for they are here to assist you in decision making and to increases your confidence. Reflect as to what your ancestors would have done in a situation; or find a spiritual master or teacher that you relate to who has passed to the other side. Allow them to guide you. Take on their wisdom and you will accomplish and meet your goals with better ease. The main thing our departed loved ones want us to know is that they are not dead; they are just not in a physical body! It is like the coffee in the cup. When the coffee has spilled and the cup broken, the cup cannot be used but the coffee is still there- just not in its old container.

23. Service to others: When we serve others we connect with their needs and we, in turn, get our needs addressed. As you give you will receive, perhaps not from where you gave, but you will receive. This raises our joy when we can give unselfishly to others.

24. Practice being generous: This is a wonderful attribute. It is important to be generous to yourself and others. There are many ways to put this principle into action. You can be generous with your love, your praise, your time, your talents, your labor, your hospitality. You can give encouragement to yourself and others. Being generous will keep you in a positive, joyous and harmonious vibration.

25. Use healing tools: There are tools that elevate and cleanse your aura, like the gentle wind project, receiving *Reiki*, energy balancing, aura cleansing with crystals, swimming in mineral waters, natural spa waters, sun and moon bathing. Use mineral baths to cleanse your aura.

26. Nurture your soul: All of the points in this chapter are intended to nurture body, mind and soul, but in this final point I wish to stress the importance of nurturing the soul within. Listen to the guidance from that inner voice, the voice of the soul, and respond in harmony with its vibration. This is a most important factor for finding and living your purpose, your dreams. This is nurturing the soul.

In this life you will live two lives. One life is experienced internally (inner world) and one externally (outer world). The external, the one you see with your eyes, is shaped by your internal life – your dreams, aspirations, thoughts and what you ingest. Choose thoughts and actions that reflect true love, that honor you, that bring joy to your very soul, for these are the keys that open all doors in the external life. These are the keys to experiencing your magnificent bloom, as a beautiful flower, in this wondrous lifetime.

"You only live twice; once in your life and once in your dreams." From James Bond 'You Only Live Twice' Song track.

Note to Self: *The Divine Creator created our magnificent design; but we use that design to create our own selves and the lives we live.*

Chapter 18:

The Happy, Grateful Body

Expressing gratitude is part of a high vibrational life. It is important to express gratitude through our words, but it is also essential to express gratitude through our actions.

I see gratitude as faith actualized, for everything that happens to us is for a reason; although sometimes those reasons are unbeknownst to us. Each reason, however, is under Divine wisdom and purpose, therefore we give gratitude for all that occurs and all that we experience. Divine wisdom and purpose guides all daily affairs. We may not fully know why, or understand why, but we trust and know it is all for good and higher vibration. This is how we keep a positive attitude.

The Gratitude Factor

Expressing gratitude gives us health in our

bones, and greater harmony flows into our lives. It is the door opener to receive our hearts' desires. Breathe in gratitude. Breathe out uncertainty.

Lying in my bed in Jamaica, I heard the most beautiful singing of the love birds. It sounded like they were saying "Thank YoUUUUUU, Thank YoUUUUUU." I began to copy them by singing the same thing. I felt wonderful. Now, whenever something throws off my emotions, I am reminded of the Love birds "Thank YoUUUU!" Then what I am experiencing does not seem so difficult.

I ask myself, "How have I shown my body that I am grateful toward it today?" The body's cells respond to gratitude. I start off by sending gratitude to my feet. I think how would my life be without my feet, then I say out loud, "I am sending love and gratitude to my feet." I feel gratitude for my feet. Then I move up to my ankles and I repeat. Then I move up to my calves, then to my knees. This gratitude exercise is very effective for energizing and healing the cells of the body.

I like to refer to Dr. Emoto's book "The Hidden Messages of Water," and his extensive research about water. In his book he describes the response of water when he spoke and displayed love messages to the water, then froze it into ice. The water then formed beautiful symmetrical ice flakes. When he cursed the water and placed the message "I hate you," it formed ill-formed crystals. Imagine, these water crystals responded to human words and vibrations.

Our bodies, being mostly water, respond in the same manner. We vibrate higher to beautiful images and we tend to avoid unpleasant images. The water within us responds to thoughts and vibrations just like the water responded to Dr. Emoto's water experiment.

There are also studies that prove children who are constantly surrounded by cursing or negative talk have a weaker immune system. Children who are subjected to a loving, caring and environment are healthier and perform better in school.

By doing the gratitude exercise daily you are reinforcing your body with positive energy, raising your immune system and creating a healthier and happier body. Show your gratitude to the Creator, the one who made your body, by taking better care of your body. Begin this and you will bring forward a new you! Begin to *LOVE YOUR BODY* and see your sickness fading away! See your disease diminishing fully! Tell the disease to go away! The *BODY* is made with such awesomeness that it will actually *HEAL ITSELF* when placed in the right conditions.

The Natural High

Feel the vibe, and then expand it. That means get in touch with your feelings. Our feelings are the gateway to our soul. Have a liberating thought; then seed it with the vision of health and wellbeing. As you breathe in remember to be conscious of your breath. Visualize what you would like to happen. Then breathe it out.

You energize the thought by breathing into it. Notice your energy. If it contracts, then breathe past it and notice how you feel. Do you feel expansion and good feelings, or a negative constriction? Notice what is there and breathe into it. Breathing says, "I accept what is, and transmute the energy into higher vibrations." Congratulations, you have just expanded your energy field. After you feel your energy field expand, seed it again with your visualizations. When you feel good, your vibrations are raised. The feelings are indicators of being "on" rather than "off."

Feelings are important indicators as to whether we are connected to our higher purpose or not. Respect your feelings, negative or positive, as they are our teachers. Whenever we try to avoid our feelings by not feeling them, they come out in other ways, such as abusing drugs, sex, and food. By processing and feeling our feelings, and transmuting them, we gain control over them. Feelings are not to control our lives but they are barometers of what is present in our lives.

Notice your skin also. It vibrates to the energy of acceptance. When you do not fully accept who you are, you may develop skin problems. I have discovered that people tend to have skin eruptions like hives, rashes and redness on the skin when holding on to past anger issues for a long time. Remember a long time can be as fast as three minutes. For that is the average time it takes bio-chemicals emitted from emotions to entirely circulate throughout the body.

Note to Self: For every moment, I
now choose to live life to the fullest.

Chapter 19:

Allowing Maximum Being

Life is simply a mirror reflection of the gateway to our very soul. The gateway will always allow the taking in of more life. I met a woman that was 83 years old. She looked like she was in her 60's. She had very little grey hair, and a big beautiful smile. She learned to trust in the unfolding of life. She had raised seven children. She had a strong faith in God.

When I visited her at her home, she was painting on a large canvas. She explained that after her kids were grown, she went to the Senior Center and learned how to paint. She learned how to paint beautiful pictures on canvas. She began painting in her fifties. She really loved it! The woman had her paintings proudly displayed and framed on the hallway walls of her eloquent home. Her home was arranged with beautiful flowers and crystal chandeliers.

What struck me most about her was her positive attitude about life. In life we all want to experience what I call "the bloom!" Like flowers, we appreciate life more when we have bloomed to maturity.

When I met this wonderful woman, she shared such great stories about her life, her challenges, her triumphs and trials. She was still smiling; she looked unfazed. Life unfolded beautifully for her and every day she participated in the creation process of painting and designing her artwork! She was a great example like a beautiful flower in full bloom!

The Big Turn-Around

I have seen the nearly dead, pain stricken, and down trodden turn their lives around after changing their diet, mindset and habits of treating the body. What you reap you have sown, and what you eat you will reap. Are you sick and tired of being sick and tired? Change old habits, what you eat, what you think, and you will change your life!

I have seen it time and time again. It happened in my own life when I was sick with cancer. I was scared and alone although people visited me every day. I was alone in the process because no one knew what to do to get me healthy again, so I began to listen to the still small voice within. It began dealing with me in regard to what I ate. I thought and visualized seeing myself healed. I prayed for healing. I began to think positive thoughts. I changed what I was drinking and eating. I turned my body, mind and soul around. I began to think higher and clearer. I became more purposeful with my time and days. I became more effective in what I wanted to create with my life.

I began creating a life by design. I lost weight. I had more energy. I began to look and feel younger.

Use It or Lose It

Condition it or lose it. Whatever we do not use, we lose. The Creator does not like something that is idle or something that has no purpose. The universe gets rid of it very quickly! For example, if shoes are not worn they begin to dry rot! If clothes are not worn they begin to get holes, and when food is not used it begins to rot. Our bodies, if not exercised, begin to get out of shape and begin to decline in strength. The good news is that anyone at any time can begin to exercise, and the body will begin to respond favorably.

Use It and Keep It

There was a woman on a popular television talk show. She was called 'ageless beauty.' She was placed behind a Plexiglas, outside on a busy sidewalk. Everyone who passed by her tried to guess her age! People were guessing fifty, fifty one, fifty nine. When the woman finally reveled her age she was 87! Unbelievable! She started exercising when she was 72!

I was very close to a woman named Edna. I had throughout the years adopted her into my family and affectionately called her 'Grandmother,' but that was not because she looked like a Grandmother. That was because of her honorable ways. She was the great example of a caring, loving human being. She was in her late sixties when I met her, and she was dedicated to her exercise and a proper diet. Years earlier, when she was fifty, she was diagnosed with heart disease and it was recommended by her doctor that she undergo open heart surgery. For, her arteries were very much blocked and this could cause a heart attack. Grandmother was an unconventional thinker and decided against the open heart surgery.

She changed her ways of thinking and her eating habits. She became a vegetarian and began practicing yoga. She lost weight she also began taking vitamin supplements. She is now in her eighties, and she looks better now and is in much better shape than when she was fifty.

Next is Jackie, who is very adventurous like me. She moved to Jamaica and developed a spa there. She did this when she was fifty. She had been a clothes designer and boutique owner in SoHo, New York City. She closed the store and began a life changing career in the spa industry. Today, Jackie looks fabulous. She looks like late forties. She looks great.

I have observed many who look fabulous with mature age, and I discovered what they do. I have also observed those who are very sick, who look very old and beyond their years, and discovered what they do. Life always rewards us with what we practice!

Jackie, now at seventy years old, snorkels, works in her spa business and exercises every day. She also practices yoga and takes supplements. She has trained herself to eat small, healthy portions. None of these ladies I mentioned has any sugar diabetes, arthritis, osteoporosis, or any debilitating illness. They live life fully every day!

You can be healthy, happy and look fabulous at any age at any time. You can start now. Make a choice. Life will reward you. Of course, have a talk with your health professional before beginning any exercise routine. Do use the help of a conscious, holistic health nutritionist when changing your diet.

The rewards are too numerous to count. Exercise always beautifies with consistency. Another way to condition the body is to keep it limber through stretching. Yoga is great for this, too. Stretch at least 5 minutes per day. Stretching keeps the body limber, allows the chi body energy to flow, and keeps the muscles toned.

PLAN it, See it, and Manifest it!

Build purpose into your days. Meditate on what you wish to accomplish, write it down and decree it. Decree a thing and it will be done to you. Fashion your days to reflect what you wish to have happen. Then go boldly and courageously in the direction you wish to go. I dreamed of living on a tropical Island. I dreamed of owning my business. I dreamt it, and then visualized it, meditated on it. Then wrote my dream down; then decreed it. It actually came to pass. I did not let money or HOW it was going to happen stop me. My thoughts were *nothing ventured, nothing gained.* Meditate means to think deeply about something.

Focus clearly on your dream and you will bring it to pass. What you think about, you bring about. Where the mind goes the body follows. Through the law of attraction, your thoughts act like a magnet, drawing to you the necessary everyday experiences. Everything you have and all you experience, came to you from your constant thoughts about it.

Whatever you deeply focus on you will manifest in your life. *As a man thinks in his heart so is he.* See yourself being happy, healthy, and balanced. You will begin to be that way. Your thoughts are important in directing your life. Everything you have in your life began as a thought. So think only on that you want to see happen. Qualify those thoughts by making them happy thoughts for you and for others, and you are sure to live a joyous and prosperous life!

I use prayer as a habit. I ask the Creator for what I want. I use gratitude, being thankful for each and every thing that happens to me. For everything that happens to me, whether negative or positive, happens to me for the good. Be 100% accountable for everything that happens in your life. Think and allow your mind to dwell only on thoughts where you want your mind to go. This is one of the great secrets in life.

Love your work, love your world, and life becomes fabulous. Your mind can make your life heaven or hell. Be true to yourself and your life's work. This is *the pursuit of the soul.*

Do not compromise your life for money. The emphasis on money is not worth the sacrifice of your happiness or your soul. For compromise can bring misery and sickness.

The real truth is the constant inquiry of what your soul is asking for. What is requires today may not be what is needed tomorrow. The key is to stay open, never frozen. Stay flexible, never concrete. Life shifts with its various angels and degrees. Be happy that it does, for this keeps the oil in the flask of the soul. The constant revolving circle of life is what is constant.

So the question is this: "What are you designing for the satisfaction of your very own soul?

This is the most important question, focused on why you are here in the first place. The soul crafts sickness and tragedy to awaken you to answer this very question.

These are gifts, but you were trained that these are curses. For, any event that occurs to awaken the soul to its true purpose is a gift, if one chooses to see it. That is why most of our challenges give us our greatest markers for positive change. Now that you have discovered this wisdom, you must make it yours. Shine it, gloss it, practice, focus, and dedicate your breath to it. Own it. It is yours and yours alone. This true diamond begins to glisten; it is the call of the soul. The real tragedy is to have a gift and never actualize it.

Conduit for the Limitless

Pamper *you*. Make *you* a priority. Your wonderful body machine needs to be treated very special. It took a lot of time and detail to create it. It has special needs for maintaining it.

Some folks take better care of their cars and animals than they do their bodies. It is your job to take care of the body that you inhabit. Since this body is the conduit for the Divine. Consider that how you treat the body is a reflection of how you think of and have appreciation for the Creator! Respect the Creator by beginning to reverence the body that was made by the Creator. When we show gratitude for what was created, we give gratitude to Source Energy.

Balancing Act

The body is balanced by detoxing the body. Read my next book, *"Detox to Fabulous,"* to get the wonderful details of cleansing the body temple. I have found that once a person eliminates the toxins from their body, not only do they feel better; the body begins to heal itself. Getting regular massages, body scrubs, facials, spa, and foot treatments are essential for keeping the body in great shape. Also, they are the best for keeping the body looking and feeling great! They de-stress and keep the body looking youthful and refreshed. Massages like therapeutic, deep-tissue, Swedish massages, are recommended for improving circulation, skin integrity, and muscle tone, and for reducing stress and cleaning the body's lymphatic system. *Acupressure point* massages, *Thai* massage, *ohasi* massage, *tui na* massage, *shitshu* massage are recommended for tuning the body's energy system.

Emotions – the Gateway for Health or Disease

Emotions are very powerful in controlling the body. Every organ in the body has a physical, emotional, and spiritual meaning to it. By understanding the physical purpose of each organ, one can connect to the spiritual and emotional meaning. The pages that follow address the key organs:

KIDNEYS: These organs are very sensitive to the water reserves in the body. They filter out impurities in the blood and keep the blood balanced with the right properties to maintain the body. Imagine, for a moment, that your kidneys are like two big washing machines for your body. What if you put your clothes in a washer, then put the soap on top of the clothes, then you turned on the washer but turned off the pipe so no water could fill the washer tub? Would you consider this a safe and practical way to wash your clothes? No, of course not, the clothes won't get clean and it may break the washer.

This, however, is what goes on in your body every day when you eat your food, or your *fod (my made up name for fake food)*, and dump a lot of salt in the body, and drink no water. Now the kidneys have to work extra hard to clean and filter the blood. After a while the kidneys get so fed up and tired of poor working conditions that they shut down. You then go to the Doctor and find that the kidneys now need dialysis.

The Kidneys can stay healthy by drinking the right kind of water on a frequent and daily basis. Have you ever tried cleaning anything without water? The inside of your body needs water to cleanse itself, just like the outside of your body.

Water cannot be substituted with anything else but water. Not water with sugar, not flavored drinks, tea, not flavored water or juices. It has to be 100% pure water. Why? How the body works: anything added to water goes through the digestive process. Water and alcohol are the only substances known that are directly absorbed through the bloodstream.

Fear keeps the kidneys off balance. I used to work with dialysis patients. These are patients that need a machine to drain the urine out of the body because their kidneys have shut down and stopped manufacturing urine on their own. This can be a lethal problem. So these patients must come in frequently and get the urine filtered out by a dialysis machine.

I would talk with them to find out the root cause of their disease. What I discovered is that the majority of these patients never liked to drink water. They tend to smoke, drink alcohol, and the underlying connection is that these patients had a lot of rooted fear and psychological abuse. Let me clarify that this type of fear is fear of living the best life. For example, these folks allowed a lot of 'what ifs' to stop them from taking chances that in their heart of hearts they knew would make them more vibrant, healthy and joyful.
This mind set of fear continuously bathes the kidneys in the energy of fear, thereby leading to kidney failure. The kidneys respond to the vibration of LOVE. The vibration of FEAR destroys the kidneys. These emotions, then, send biochemical reactions to your body that have a profound connection with your health.

Kidney affirmation: *I now release fear and allow love to flow.* Repeat three times silently and visualize water flowing freely from your kidneys to your bladder and releasing out.

LUNGS: The lungs process the air we breathe and convert it into a substance that can be absorbed into the blood stream. Your lungs correspond to taking in the fullness of life. The energies of depression and grief are the emotions that can cause lung problems. Grief keeps the lungs off balance. Asthma is also

212

a communicator that tells us the power of life is impaired!

Lungs affirmation: *I am happy and free; I take in life fully!*

HEART: The heart is the center of our emotional and spiritual wellbeing. Through our speaking and actions, the heart reflects to the world who and what we really are within. Are we happy, joyful, peaceful, and content? Or are we angry, jealous, fearful or dejected? The heart reflects to the external what we hold in the internal. The heart also measures sincerity and trust of ourselves and others. When trust is broken, the resulting human emotions affect the heart. These emotions can cause stress, heart attacks and heart disease.

Heart affirmation: Breathe in deeply while you repeat this three times out loud: *I allow trust, joy and love of myself to unfold freely.*

STOMACH: The stomach accepts foods, and digests and assimilates nutrients for the body; but on an emotional level, the stomach accepts ideas, concepts, and situations. Emotionally, it is quick to feel and accept and put meaning into life's circumstances. A troubled or upset stomach can be an emotional reaction as well as a food reaction.

Stomach affirmation: . I accept my life's circumstances as being whole and complete.

SPLEEN/PANCREAS: These related organs break down blood cells and process foods. The spleen stays healthy when the body is experiencing happiness. A lack of joy or extreme unhappiness keeps the

213

spleen off balance. Sugar diabetes is formed from constant unhappiness and lack of joy. My Grandfather left my Grandmother for another woman, one of her close friends as a matter of fact. Shortly after my Grandfather left, my Grandmother developed sugar diabetes. Then I saw her undergo a lot of adverse changes. She endured a heart attack, not one, but three. The third one was fatal.

The spleen and pancreas are essential for filtering out impurities in the body, and are especially important for removing toxins from the blood and other vital organs.

We renew and energize our spleen and pancreas vibrations by keeping a positive attitude. It is important to hold your vibration for a light for yourself, and to turn negatives into positive, reversing how you might have seen a negative situation. I think of a soiled baby. All you want to do is clean the baby up, perhaps put some nice powder on him and a fresh diaper. Then you say," There you go baby, all fresh again." Why don't we look at our mishaps and mistakes like the baby who needs a diaper change? Take care of what is soiled and move on! Take something that has not been pleasing you, or making you unhappy, and make it all fresh again by seeing it in a new light! We don't love the baby less because he soils a diaper, for we realize he does not know any better.

Spleen/Pancreas affirmation: *I allow my life to come to me with joy and glory.*

LIVER: The liver's job is to clean the blood and body fluids. The liver's efficiency, however, is adversely affected by the vibration or emotions of anger and unresolved aggression. Depression and angry feelings can arise from the body being laden with toxic chemicals and artificial foods! They are so denatured we cannot call them food.

If you notice you are angry a lot, begin to start eating high water based foods like soups, lettuce, watermelon, pumpkin. These healing foods help the liver to cleanse and balance itself.

Liver affirmations: *I allow love in and release anger. I allow love to balance my vibrations.* See pink light enveloping the anger. Love flowing into you on every inhalation. Repeat three times.

GALLBLADDER: This organ produces gall or bile, a digestive liquid that breaks down fats and greasy foods, and neutralizes acids. Emotionally is affected by deep resentment and frustration.

Gallbladder affirmation: *I now love and forgive everyone, myself included.*

ENDOCRINE GLANDS: Endocrine glands are the body's timing system. The endocrine glands regulate specific functions of the body, such as sleep and awake cycles and menstrual cycles in women. These glands function and monitor cycles by receiving signals from the brain. Endocrine glands include the pineal gland, the pituitary gland, the thyroid, parathyroid gland, thymus gland, adrenal gland, pancreas, testes and ovaries.

Endocrine glands affirmation: *I am in the perfect flow and timing of life.*

SMALL INTESTINE: This organ is important

for digestion. It receives food that is broken down by the digestive action of the stomach, and absorbs nutrients for distribution throughout the body. It can be adversely affected by stress and impacted by the residue of unnatural, foodless foods.

Small Intestine affirmation: *I accept and go with the flow of life.*

LARGE INTESTINE: This intestine contains waste products for elimination from the body. Holding on to old and past hurts can adversely affect this organ. It can suffer from physical as well as emotional constipation.

Large Intestine affirmation: *I now release and let go of old hurts. All things work together for my highest life purpose.*

Our Body: A Marvelous Third Dimensional Machine

The brief overview of key organs, as noted above, gives us further insight into our marvelous third dimensional presence. We are truly an intricate holographic machine that receives subtle and direct information from all universal sources.

Every thought you think creates a bio-chemical reaction in your body. 'Emotions' are *Energies in Motion*, which direct the ever-flowing life force. Your wonderful body machine, right now, is receiving and processing more information than you can consciously grasp.

Your internal thermostat regulator is picking up how hot or cold the room is, or the outside weather conditions. Your skin is measuring the tightness or looseness of your clothing. Your body is growing hair, skin cell, and other organ cells. Your eyes are registering how much light is filtering through your eyes. Your body is registering how much food you have eaten or if you are hungry.

Scientists generally concur that every three weeks you get a new stomach lining. Every six months you get a new liver. Every seven years you get a totally new body. Yet, your face and body looks somewhat the same because your cells have memory capabilities. These cells remember what they used to look like before.

So if these cells are constantly renewing, why does a disease in the cells continue through the cell transformation? One reason is your beliefs. You believe you have the disease so you continually create or preserve it by the power of your thoughts; through the law of attraction. Also, if your diet and habits that caused the disease remain the same, the disease will continue. When everything is the same, the same outcome is created. So, the body will keep the same sickness.

The body is made to eliminate non-functioning cells, which it does all the while; but those cells are replaced with new cells that retain the *'I am sick'* message and belief.

When you have sickness, change your beliefs, a negative environment, your eating and drinking habits. Begin to eat wholesome foods, begin to take supplements, begin to drink pure water, and begin to call those things that trouble you as though they are not. This will keep your body flowing at an optimal level.

Here is the key to long life; love yourself. The more *you* love *you*- the more the universe will respond with more love to and for *you*. What you broadcast is what you will get back.

"To learn is to read, to know is to write, and to master is to teach." Selma Williams

What I Want, I Create and Become

Releasing judgment of self and others is important. You can judge circumstances, but is best not to judge others or yourself too harshly. The bible says "judge not lest you be judged." Also, you who are without sin cast the first stone.

Judging others and ourselves only makes us feel badly. What I mean about judging is making yourself or others wrong. We are who we are, and others are who they are. It is through gaining complete acceptance that we truly are empowered to heal mentally and physically.

Others are our Mirrors

It is wisdom to understand that we also have the same personality traits or habits that that we like or dislike in others. They are our mirrors. What we like or dislike may be a conscious or subconscious trait within us. The only reason it bothers us, or we get a reaction when we observe it in others, is because it is somewhere in us too.

Use these observations and occurrences as tools to learn more about ourselves. If we can identify traits in others, then what we identified is also in us. What we do not like in others is what we do not like about ourselves. What we like in others is what we like about ourselves.

Our Inner Knowing... and Doing

Maya Angelou, the great and famous poet, once said, "When we know better, we do better."

It is not an intellectual knowing, not like you think you know better because someone told you so, or you think it is so. It is an inner knowing that is a conviction beyond a shadow of a doubt.

We humans are made to automatically do what is better when we understand and are convicted in our heart as to what is better. For example, within our mechanism is a desire to always seek pleasure and avoid pain. When we fully understand that our behavior is causing pain, we are created to seek to avoid it. If we understand a particular behavior creates pleasure, we will seek to continue it. The key is to understand the long term effects of our behavior when it comes to our health and longevity.

For example, understanding that consistent negative emotions adversely affect our organs will encourage us to master negative emotions. This is a central purpose of this book. I want readers to understand the long term effects that particular ways of thinking and behaving have on the body's health.

A Time for Positive Change

We tend to attract into our lives people, things,

and situations that vibrate on our level. So we must ask ourselves if we are satisfied with where we are in life. What are our goals? Want to lose weight? Want to get in shape? Want to be healed? Want to renew youth? Get a stronger body? Want to get limber? Want to change an uncomfortable environment? The body is made and functions within certain principles and universal laws. Your thoughts are vibrational tuning forks. The environment is an out picturing of your consistent beliefs and thoughts. Use your thoughts to re-direct your life and change your environment to one that is higher vibrational.

Focus and continue to focus until you manifest what you desire. What you think about, you bring about. What you focus on expands. The body always follows the mind.

I encourage you to break through the self-imposed mental and physical restraints and limitations. What you generate or 'put into' life is what you will get out of your human experience.

"The whole point of being alive is to evolve into the person you are meant to be." Oprah Winfrey.

Note to Self: *I love you; therefore I take care of you - all of you!*

Chapter 20:

The Art
of Ascension

The mind and body are deeply connected. The mind's thoughts and beliefs shape our physical experiences. These are actually mind-body experiences.

What you believe you will create in the physical. The health of the body is an outward expression of the workings of the mind. With intention of the mind, the body can regenerate and continue to get better not weaker.

Observing our Healing

All things change over time, because energy is constantly flowing and changing. A key to good health is the observation of these changes. What might have benefited you yesterday, may no longer work the same today. Health, like life, is dynamic and constantly changing like the hands of a clock. Time is also changing your body and how it functions. But, time can be your friend, and not your enemy. For, all things work together for perfection. The key to health is to observe changes, and know what works as changes come.

You are not your mind; you are not your body. You are a spirit holding residence in your body and your mind. Since you are not your mind, the thoughts that pass through your mind are to be observed as having truth and importance, or not having truth and importance. Not all thoughts that pass through the mind are truthful thoughts.

Thoughts need to be weighed for importance and validity. Ask yourself, when a thought comes through your mind, "Is this true? Is this relevant for me?" Then focus on those thoughts that have merit. Think on those thoughts that are uplifting and raise your vibration to the highest level. The quality of your thoughts are equal to the quality of your life.

Imagine you are playing musical chairs with your thoughts. If the thought is empowering, sit in the chair, dwell with that thought. If it is a criticizing, disempowering thought, let it go, change chairs. Change your thoughts, you will change your vibration. Change your vibration, you will change your destiny. Change your destiny, and you will change your life!

The Tree

There were some tree cutters sawing down a huge oak tree on a residential street. The tree had simply grown too large and was now causing the city some maintenance problems. It was affecting power lines and the concrete sidewalk was bulging and cracking from its huge roots.

The persons cutting the tree down were zealous and rushing to get the job done. There was a loud, thunderous crack as the tree snapped and twisted under enormous weight. The great oak fell, but crashed down upon a house instead of falling into the street as the tree cutter had originally planned. The effect seemed disastrous as the homeowner, who luckily was not home at the time, learned later that he had lost his home.

The mayor, however, after being informed of the mishap, ordered the city to not only restore the man's home, but build a brand new home, bigger and better than the original. What appeared to be disastrous at the time, turned out to be a great blessing as the homeowner received an upgrade to everything he had owned in the house as well.

Is this happy ending rare? No, life is like that, full of wonderful possibilities. What originally can appear disastrous, can turn out to be a blessing and an upgrade in life. We must be willing to accept the circumstances. Then look for and create the upgrade. We do this by the 'T.W.V.P.P.P Method':

Think about it;
Write it down;
Visualize it;
Put Practices into Place to achieve the results.

A Catalyst for Change

I am a catalyst for change and wellbeing. I wish

to introduce to you a new set of ways, thoughts, and beliefs to shift what you are or have gone through in your past.

A wise person said insanity is doing the same thing and expecting different results. If what you have been doing has not worked for you, I encourage you to try something different. Look for new ways of creating the best life possible for yourself and others.

I know that all things are possible to the one who believes! I have had enough miracles, and have witnessed enough miracles in others, to confirm this. The main *pursuit of the soul* is to be happy by expressing one's divine purpose here on Earth. You are here to find your own unique purpose and express it happily. Fullness of joy and peace of mind are the fruits of happy, full, wondrous self-expression.

Note to Self: I take my life to the next level; and to the next; and to the next and the next... like the unfolding of a beautiful flower in full bloom.

Dear reader, if you have questions or comments you may email me. I will be happy to discuss any aspect of wellness for body, mind and soul.

Avery Alexander (SaEnya)
saenya@yahoo.com

Reference Book List

"The Miracle of Mind Power" by Dan Custer

"The Eye of the I from which Nothing is Hidden" by David R. Hawkins, MD, PHD

"You Can Have it All" by Arnold Patent

"Chakras Energy Centers of Transformation" by Harish Johari

"Think on these Things" by Edgar Cayce

"A Day of Grace" by Michael Lightweaver

"Fasting for Health and Long Life" by Hereward Carrington, PhD

"Basic Herbs for Health and Healing" by Rashan Abdul Hakim

"Notes on Nursing" by Florence Nightengale

"Indian Uses of Native Plants" by Edith Van Allen Murphy, (Meyerbrooks, Glenwwod, Illinois,USA 60425) 1958, 1987, 1990

"Natural Healing with Herbs" by Humbart Santilo, (Holm Press, Prescott Valley, Arizona, USA) 1985

"Wheels of Life" Anodea Judith, (Liewwe;yn Publication, Minnesota, USA) 1987

"Natural Healing with Herbs" by Humbart Santillo

"Hands of Light" by Barbara Brennan

"The Key to Yourself" by Dr. Venice Bloodworth

"Creative Visualizations" by Shakti Gwain

"The Ekklesia" by Arthur A. Ferdig

"The Spirit in our Clay" by Arthur A. Ferdig

"The Seven Spiritual Laws of Success" by Depak Chopra

"You're It" by Kay Latham Slesinger-Rich

"Intention" by Dr. Wayne Dyer

"Teachings of Abraham" by Abraham Hicks

"You can Heal Your Life" by Louise Hay

"How to Meditate in 30 Minutes" by Ra Un Nefer Amen

"Healing the Errors of Living" by Ra Un Nefer Amen

"Het Heru Dance" by Queen Mast Aum Amen

"You Can Have it All" by Arnold Patent

"Vitamins from A to Z" By Dr. Jewel Pookrum

"Juicing" By Cherie Cheelblom

The information is this book was written to share the author's true experiences, her own observations, and those of her patients and clients.

This book was NOT written or intended to treat, or diagnose any diseases. The author recommends that one always consults with a qualified healthcare professional for diagnosis, guidance or recommended treatment.

Made in the USA
Columbia, SC
21 July 2022

63728858R00136